D. E. Richards.

Mo. Uni. Mar. 12 1869

THE

ROMANCE OF M. RENAN,

AND THE

CHRIST OF THE GOSPELS.

Three Essays

BY

REV. DR. SCHAFF AND M. NAPOLEON ROUSSEL.

NEW YORK:
CARLTON & LANAHAN.
CINCINNATI: HITCHCOCK & WALDEN.
TRACT SOCIETY OF THE METHODIST EPISCOPAL CHURCH,
1868.

NOTE BY THE AMERICAN EDITOR.*

THIS work is reprinted from the London Religious Tract Society's edition. The same reasons which made its publication desirable in England apply to American society. For, though M. Renan's work may not be very generally read among us, yet its thought and spirit are being largely reproduced by the Rationalistic pulpit and press,—the latter especially. Hencc it is necessary to provide a popular antidote for what may be regarded as popular poison. This little volume is such an antidote. PROFESSOR SCHAFF'S

* The title of the second essay of this volume has been placed first, to prevent the work from being confounded with "The Christ of the Gospels" by Tulloch, published by our Western Book Concern.

Essay brings out the true character of the Christ of the Gospels in such bold relief, and with such convincing evidence, as to arm its reader's mind against the insidious weapons of Strauss and Renan. M. Roussel's two Essays grapple boldly and strongly with the false principles on which the work of Renan is constructed. Any man, after carefully considering them, would find it difficult to yield his assent to the plausible positions of that adversary of the Lord Jesus. I particularly commend these pages to young preachers and to young men, whether they have read Renan's work or not; assured, that if they have read it, and have even had their faith shaken, the argument and views herein contained will be likely to restore their faith in the real Christ; while, if they have not read it, they will here see enough of its character to convince them that its aim is evil, and that, like all other weapons heretofore forged by the skill of skepticism against the Holy Child Jesus, it is sure to be soon buried in everlasting contempt.

D. W.

PREFACE.

THE *Vie de Jesus*, by M. Renan, having passed through many editions, and been translated into several languages on the continent of Europe, has now appeared in an English form. The Committee of the Religious Tract Society have therefore deemed it incumbent upon them to provide some antidote to the errors of a volume which is being so widely circulated. At the same time they do not think that M. Renan's treatise either needs or deserves a formal reply. It adduces no new facts and urges no new arguments against the Christian faith. It is not remarkable either for depth of research or vigor of logic. It owes its sudden and wonderful popularity, not to its intrinsic merit, but to the beauty of its style and the position of its author. All the reasonings which have been so successfully urged against other skeptical treatises may be adduced with equal force against this; and it lies open to many objections peculiar to itself. The admissions which M. Renan has felt himself compelled to make in favor of Christianity are fatal to his arguments against it. He admits the early origin, the authenticity, and the general veracity of the Gospels; yet he rejects all the miracles which they record, and reduces their narratives to fabulous and mythical legends as often as it suits his purpose. He admits that Jesus was the wisest, holiest, and best of the sons of men; yet he pities him as the victim of delusion, and apologizes for him as the accessory to, or the accomplice in, acts of imposture and fraud. He admits that Christianity has been the great means of the world's progress in the past, and that it holds out the only hope for the world's progress in the future; yet he maintains that it was founded in fanaticism, and that it is strong only by its faith in a delusion. These absurdities, indeed, do not appear on the surface of the book. They are ingeniously vailed by glowing descriptions and paraphrastic statements.

It has been thought sufficient, therefore, to place in the hands of English readers the following essays.

1. A treatise, by the Rev. Professor Schaff,* on the Christ of the Gospels, in which the perfection of our Lord's character, as portrayed by the Evangelists, is set forth as an argument for the Divinity of his person and mission. A character so spotless and perfect, yet so simple and natural, could not be the product of imposture, or the dream of fanaticism. In the words of Rousseau, "It is more inconceivable that a number of persons should agree to write such a history, than that one only should furnish the subject of it. The Jewish authors were incapable of the diction, and strangers to the morality contained in the Gospels, the marks of whose truth are so striking and

* Reprinted, with revision and additions, from the "British and Foreign Evangelical Review."

inimitable that the inventor would be even a more astonishing character than the hero." As this essay was written before the appearance of the *Vie de Jesus,* it has been thought desirable to add a few notes pointing out its bearing upon the work of M. Renan.

2. Two essays, by M. Napoleon Roussel, one of the ablest of the French Protestant pastors, in which the insidious and latent principles of the *Vie de Jesus* are stripped of their disguise, and laid bare in their naked deformity. Many who might be deluded and seduced by the rhetorical romance of M. Renan would start back with horror from an unvailed statement of his teachings.

These essays are published with the earnest prayer that they may be made instrumental in leading many not only to reject the evil, but to choose the good. It is not enough to detect the sophisms and repudiate the conclusions of infidelity, unless, at the same time, "being justified by faith, we have peace with God through our Lord Jesus Christ."

CONTENTS.

THE

CHRIST OF THE GOSPELS.

BY REV. PROFESSOR SCHAFF.

THE

CHRIST OF THE GOSPELS.

THE life and character of Jesus Christ is truly the Holy of Holies in the history of the world. Eighteen hundred years have passed away since he, in the fullness of time, appeared on this earth to redeem a fallen race from sin and death, and to open a never-ceasing fountain of righteousness and life. The ages before him anxiously awaited his coming as "the Desire of all nations;" the ages after him proclaim his glory, and ever extend his dominion. The noblest and best of men under every clime hold him not only in the purest affection and the profoundest gratitude, but in divine adoration and worship. His name is above every name that can be named in heaven or on earth, and the only one whereby the sinner can be saved. He is Immanuel, God with us; the eternal Word become flesh, very God and very man in one undivided person; the Author of the new creation; the Way, the Truth, and the Life; the Prophet, Priest, and King of regenerate humanity; the Saviour of the world. Thus he stands out to the faith of the entire Christian Church, Greek, Latin, and Evangelical, in every civilized country on the globe. His power is now greater, his kingdom larger, than ever, and will continue to spread until all nations shall bow before him, and kiss his scepter of righteousness and peace.

Blessed is he who, from the heart, can believe that Jesus is the Son of God and the fountain of salvation. True faith is, indeed, no work of nature, but an act of God wrought in the soul by the Holy Ghost, who reveals Christ to us in his true character, as Christ revealed the Father. Faith, with its justifying, sanctifying, and saving power, is independent of science and learning, and may be kindled even in the heart of a little child or an illiterate slave. It is the peculiar glory of the Redeemer and his religion to be coextensive with humanity itself, without distinction of sex, age, condition, nation, and race. His saving grace flows and overflows to all, and for all, on the simple condition of repentance and faith.

This fact, however, does not supersede the necessity of thought and argument. Revelation, although above nature and above reason, is by no means against nature and against reason. On the contrary, nature and the supernatural, as has been well said by a distinguished New England divine, (Bushnell,) "constitute together the one system of God." Christianity satisfies the deepest intellectual as well as moral and religious wants of man, who is created in the image, and for the glory of God. It is the revelation of truth as well as of life. Faith and knowledge are not antagonistic, but complementary forces; not enemies, but inseparable twin sisters. Faith, indeed, precedes knowledge, but it just as necessarily leads to knowledge; while true knowledge, on the other hand, is always rooted and grounded in faith, and tends to confirm and strengthen it. Thus we find the two combined in the famous confession of Peter, when he says in the name of all the other apostles, "We *believe* and *are sure* that thou art that Christ."

As living faith in Christ is the soul and center of all sound practical Christianity and piety, so the true doctrine of Christ is the soul and center of all sound Christian theology. St. John makes the denial of the incarnation of the Son of God the criterion of Antichrist, and consequently the belief in this central truth the test of Christianity. The incarnation, and the Divine glory shining through the vail of Christ's humanity, is the grand theme of his Gospel, which he wrote, as with the pen of an angel, from the very heart of Christ, as his favorite disciple and bosom friend. The Apostles' Creed, starting as it does from the confession by Peter, makes the article on Christ most prominent, and assigns to it the central position between the preceding article of God the Father and the succeeding article on the Holy Ghost. The development of ancient catholic theology commenced and culminated with the triumphant defense of the true Divinity and true humanity of Christ against the opposite heresies of Judaizing Ebionism which denied the former, and paganizing Gnosticism which resolved the latter into a shadowy phantom. The evangelical Protestant theology is essentially Christological, or controlled throughout by the proper idea of Christ as the God-man and Saviour. This is emphatically "the article of the standing or falling Church." In this, the two most prominent ideas of the Reformation, the doctrine of the supremacy of the Scriptures, and the doctrine of justification by grace through faith, meet and are vitally united. Christ's word, the only unerring and sufficient guide of truth; Christ's work, the only unfailing and sufficient source of peace; Christ all in all—this is the principle of genuine Protestantism.

In the construction of the true doctrine of Christ's person, we may, with St. John in the prologue to his Gospel, begin from above with his eternal Godhead, and proceed through the creation and the preparatory revelation of the Old Testament dispensation, till we reach the incarnation and his truly human life for the redemption of the race. Or, with the other Evangelists, we may begin from below, with his birth from the Virgin Mary, and rise up through the successive stages of his earthly life, his discourses and miracles, to his assumption into that Divine glory which he had before the foundation of the world. The result reached in both cases is the same, that Christ unites in his person the whole fullness of the Godhead and the whole fullness of sinless manhood.

The older theologians, both Catholic and Evangelical, proved the divinity of the Saviour in a direct way from the miracles performed by him, and the prophecies fulfilled in him, from the Divine names which he bears, from the Divine attributes which are predicted of him, from the Divine works which he performed, and from the Divine honors which he claimed, and which were freely accorded to him by his Apostles and the whole Christian Church to this day.

But it may also be proved by the opposite process—the contemplation of the singular perfection of his humanity, which rises, by the almost universal consent even of unbelievers, so far above every human greatness known before or since, that it can only be rationally explained on the ground of such an essential union with the Godhead as he claimed himself, and as his inspired Apostles ascribed to him. The more deeply we penetrate through the vail of his flesh, the more clearly we behold the glory of the Only Begotten of the Father shining through it full of grace and of truth.

Modern evangelical theology owes this new homage to the Saviour. The powerful attacks of the latest phase of infidelity upon the credibility of the Gospel history call for it, and have already led, by way of reaction, to new triumphs of the old faith of the Church in her Divine Head. Our humanitarian, philanthropic, and yet skeptical age, is more susceptible of this argument than of the old dogmatic method of demonstration. With Thomas, the representative of honest and earnest skepticism among the Apostles, it refuses to believe in the divinity of the Lord unless supported by the testimony of its senses; it desires to put the finger into the print of the nails, and to thrust the hand into his side, before it exclaims in humble adoration, "My Lord and my God."

It is from this point of view that we will endeavor, in as popular and concise a manner as the difficulty of the subject permits, to analyze and exhibit the human character of Christ. We propose to take up the man Jesus of Nazareth as he appears on the simple, unsophisticated record of the plain and honest fishermen of Galilee, and as he lives in the faith of all Christendom; and we shall find him in all the stages of his life, both as a private individual and as a public character, so far elevated above the reach of successful rivalry, and so singularly perfect, that this very perfection in the midst of an imperfect and sinful world constitutes an irresistible proof of his Divinity.

A full discussion of the subject would require us to consider Christ in his official as well as personal character, and to describe him as a teacher, a reformer, a worker of miracles, and the founder of a spiritual kingdom, universal in extent and perpetual in time. From every point of view we should be irresistibly driven to the same result. But our present purpose confines us to the consideration of his personal character; and this alone, we think, is sufficient for the conclusion.

Christ passed through all the stages of human life, from infancy to manhood, and represented each in its ideal form, that he might redeem and sanctify them all, and be a perpetual model for imitation. He was the model infant, the model boy, the model youth, and the model man. But the weakness, decline, and decrepitude of old age would be incompatible with his character and mission. He died and rose in the full bloom of early manhood, and lives in the hearts of his people in unfading freshness and unbroken vigor for ever.

Let us first glance at the infancy and boyhood of the Saviour. The history of the race commences with the beauty of innocent youth in the garden of Eden, "when the morning stars sang together, and all the sons of God shouted for joy," in beholding Adam and Eve created in the image of their Maker, the crowning glory of all his wonderful works. So the second Adam, the Redeemer of the fallen race, the Restorer and Perfecter of man, comes first before us in the accounts of the Gospels as a child born, not in paradise, it is true, but among the dreary ruins of sin and death, from a humble virgin, in a lowly manger, yet pure and innocent, the subject of the praise of angels and the object of the adoration of men. Heaven and earth, the shepherds of Bethlehem, in the name of Israel, longing after salvation, and the wise men from the East, as the representatives of heathenism in its dark groping after the "unknown God," unite in the worship of the new-born King and Saviour. Here we meet, at the very threshold of the earthly history of Christ, that singular combination of humility and grandeur, of simplicity and sublimity, of the human and Divine, which characterizes it throughout, and distinguishes it from every other history. He is not represented as an unnatural prodigy, anticipating the maturity of a later age, but as a truly human child, silently lying and smiling on the bosom of his virgin mother, "growing" in body and "waxing strong in spirit," and therefore subject to the law of regular development, yet differing from all other children by his supernatural conception and perfect freedom from hereditary sin and guilt. He appears in the celestial beauty of unspotted innocence, a veritable flower of paradise. He was "that holy thing," according to the announcement of the angel Gabriel, admired and loved by all who approached him in child-like spirit, but exciting the dark suspicion of the tyrant king, who represented his future enemies and persecutors. Who can measure the ennobling, purifying, and cheering influence which proceeds from the contemplation of the Christ-child at each returning Christmas season upon the hearts of young and old in every land and nation! The loss of the first estate is richly compensated by the undying innocence of paradise regained.

Of the boyhood of Jesus we know only one fact, recorded by Luke, but it is in perfect keeping with the peculiar charm of his childhood, and foreshadows at the same time the glory of his public life, as one uninterrupted service of his heavenly Father. When twelve years old we find him in the temple, in the midst of the Jewish doctors, not teaching and offending them, as in the Apocryphal Gospels, by any immodesty or forwardness, but hearing and asking questions, thus actually learning from them, and yet filling them with astonishment at his understanding and answers. There is nothing premature, forced, or unbecoming his age, and yet a degree of wisdom and an intensity of interest in religion which rises far above a purely human youth. "He increased," we are told, "in wisdom and stature, and in favor with God and man." He was subject to his parents, and practiced all the virtues of an obedient son;* and yet he filled them with a sacred awe as they saw him absorbed "in the things of his Father," and heard him utter words which they were unable to understand at the time, but which Mary treasured up in her heart as a holy secret, convinced that they must have some deep meaning answering to the mystery of his supernatural conception and birth. Such an idea of a harmless and faultless heavenly childhood, of a growing, learning, and

* With an almost incredible untruthfulness, M. Renan quotes the narrative of Luke as a "legend which delights to show Jesus, even from his infancy, in revolt against parental authority, and departing from the common way to fulfill his vocation. It is certain, at least, that he cared little for the relations of kinship. His family do not seem to have loved him, and at times he seems to have been hard toward them." This is not to write history, but to contradict it.—Ed. R. T. S.

yet surprisingly wise boyhood, as meets us in living reality at the portal of the Gospel history, never entered the imagination of biographer, poet, or philosopher before.

The unnatural exaggeration into which the mythical fancy of man, in its endeavor to produce a superhuman childhood and boyhood, will inevitably fall, is strikingly exhibited in the Apocryphal Gospels, which are related to the Canonical Gospels as the counterfeit to the genuine coin, or as a revolting caricature to the inimitable original, but which by the very contrast tend, negatively, to corroborate the truth of the evangelical history. While the Evangelists expressly reserve the performance of miracles to the age of maturity and public life, and observe a significant silence concerning the parents of Jesus, the Pseudo-evangelists fill the infancy and early years of the Saviour and his mother with the strangest prodigies, and make the active intercession of Mary very prominent throughout. According to their representation, even dumb idols, irrational beasts, and senseless trees, bow in adoration before the infant Jesus on his journey to Egypt; and after his return, when yet a boy of five or seven years, he changes balls of clay into flying birds for the amusement of his playmates, strikes terror round about him, dries up a stream of water by a mere word, transforms his companions into goats, raises the dead to life, and performs all sorts of miraculous cures, through a magical influence which proceeds from the very water in which he was washed, the towels which he used, and the bed on which he slept. Here we have the falsehood and absurdity of unnatural fiction, while the New Testament presents to us the truth and beauty of a supernatural, yet most real history, which shines out only in brighter colors by the contrast of the mythical shadow.

With the exception of these few but significant hints, the youth of Jesus, and the preparation for his public ministry, are enshrined in mysterious silence. But we know the outward condition and circumstances under which he grew up; and these must be admitted to furnish no explanation for the astounding results, without the admission of the supernatural and Divine element in his life.

He grew up among a people seldom, and only contemptuously, named by the ancient classics, and subjected at the time to the yoke of a foreign oppressor; in a remote and conquered province of the Roman empire; in the darkest district of Palestine; in a little country town of proverbial insignificance; in poverty and manual labor; in the obscurity of a carpenter's shop; far away from universities, academies, libraries, and literary or polished society; without any help, as far as we know, except the parental care, the book of nature, the Old Testament Scriptures, and the secret intercourse of his soul with the heavenly Father. Hence the question of Nathaniel, "Can any good thing come out of Nazareth?" Hence the natural surprise of the Jews, who knew all his human relations and antecedents. "How knoweth this man letters," they asked, when they heard Jesus teach in the synagogue, "having never learned?" And on another occasion: "Whence hath this man this wisdom, and these mighty works? Is not this the carpenter's son? is not his mother called Mary? and his brethren, James, and Joses, and Simon, and Judas? And his sisters, are they not all with us? Whence then hath this man all these things?" These questions are unavoidable and unanswerable, if Christ be regarded as a mere man. For each effect presupposes a corresponding cause.

The difficulty here presented can by no means be solved by a reference to the fact that many, perhaps the majority of great men, especially in the Church, have risen by their own industry and perseverance from the lower walks of life, and from a severe contest with poverty and obstacles of every kind. The fact itself is readily conceded; but in every one of these cases, schools, or books, or patrons and friends, or peculiar events and influences, can be pointed out as auxiliary aids in the development of intellectual or moral greatness. There is always some human or natural cause, or combination of causes, which accounts for the final result.

Luther, for instance, was indeed the son of poor peasants, and had a very hard youth; but yet he went to the schools of Mansfield, Magdeburg, and Eisenach, to the University of Erfurt, passed through the ascetic discipline of convent life, lived in a university surrounded by professors, students, and libraries, and was innocently, as it were, made a reformer by extraordinary events, and the irresistible current of his age.

In the case of Christ, no such natural explanation can be given. All the attempts to bring him into some contact with Egyptian wisdom, or with the Essenic theosophy, or other sources of learning, are without a shadow of proof, and explain nothing after all. For, unlike all other great men, even the Prophets and the Apostles, he was absolutely original and independent. He taught the world as one who had learned from it, and was under no obligation to it. "His character and life were originated and sustained in spite of circumstances with which no earthly force could have contended, and therefore must have had their real foundation in a force which was preternatural and divine." At the same time, it is easy to see, from the admission of Christ's Divinity, that by this condescension he has raised humble origin, poverty, manual labor, and the lower orders of society, to a dignity and sacredness never known before, and has revolutionized the false standard of judging the value of men and things from their outward appearance, and of associating moral worth with social elevation, and moral degradation with low rank.

We now approach the public life of Jesus. In his thirtieth year, after the Messianic inauguration through the baptism by John,* as his

* Few passages in the "Vie de Jésus" will be read with more surprise than those in which M. Renan treats on the baptism of our Lord. He maintains that Jesus "was already a somewhat renowned teacher when he came to John." Almost with the air of a discovery he announces that it is by an error

immediate forerunner and personal representative of the Old Testament, both in its legal and prophetic, or evangelical aspect, and after the Messianic probation by the temptation in the wilderness—the counterpart of the temptation of the first Adam in paradise—he entered upon his great work.

His public life lasted only three years, and before he had reached the age of ordinary maturity he died in the full beauty and vigor of early manhood, without tasting the infirmities of declining years, which would inevitably mar the picture of the Regenerator of the race, and the Prince of life. And yet, unlike all other men of his years, he combined with the freshness, energy, and originating power of youth that wisdom, moderation, and experience which belong only to mature age. The short triennium of his public ministry contains more, even from

that "we imagine John to be an old man; he was, on the contrary, of the same age as Jesus;" and he dismisses "all the details of the narrative, especially those which refer to the relationship of John to Jesus, as legendary." For this we have no other authority alleged than M. Renan' s*ipse dixit.*—Ed. R. T. S.

a purely historical point of observation, than the longest life of the greatest and best of men. It is pregnant with the deepest meaning respecting the counsel of God and the destiny of the race. It is the ripe fruit of all preceding ages, the fulfillment of the hopes and desires of the Jewish and heathen mind, and the fruitful germ of succeeding generations, containing the impulse to the purest thoughts and noblest actions down to the end of time. It is "the end of a boundless past, the center of a boundless present, and the beginning of a boundless future."

How remarkable, how wonderful this contrast between the short duration and the immeasurable significance of Christ's ministry! The Saviour of the world a youth!

Other men require a long succession of years to mature their mind and character, and to make a lasting impression upon the world. There are rare exceptions, we admit. Alexander the Great, the last and most brilliant efflorescence of the ancient Greek nationality, died a young man of thirty-three, after having conquered the East to the borders of the Indus. But who would think of comparing an ambitious warrior, conquered by his own lust and dying a victim of his passion, with the spotless Friend of sinners; a few bloody victories of the one with the peaceful triumphs of the other; and a huge military empire of force, which crumbled to pieces as soon as it was erected, with the spiritual kingdom of truth and love which stands to this day, and will last forever? Nor should it be forgotten, that the true significance and only value of Alexander's conquests lay beyond the horizon of his ambition and intention, and that, by carrying the language and civilization of Greece to Asia, and bringing together the oriental and occidental world, it prepared the way for the introduction of the universal religion of Christ.

There is another striking distinction, of a general character, between Christ and the heroes of history, which we must mention here. We should naturally suppose that such an uncommon personage, setting up the most astounding claims and proposing the most extraordinary work, would surround himself with extraordinary circumstances, and maintain a position far above the vulgar and degraded multitude around him. We should expect something uncommon and striking in his look, his dress, his manner, his mode of speech, his outward life, and the train of his attendants. But the very reverse is the case. His greatness is singularly unostentatious, modest, and quiet; and far from repelling the beholder, it attracts and invites him to familiar approach. His public life never moved on the imposing arena of secular heroism, but within the humble circle of every-day life, and the simple relations of a son, a brother, a citizen, a teacher, and a friend. He had no army to command, no kingdom to rule, no prominent station to fill, no worldly favors and rewards to dispense. He was a humble individual, without friends and patrons in the Sanhedrim or at the court of Herod. He never mingled in familiar intercourse with the religious or social leaders of the nation, whom he had startled, in his twelfth year, by his questions and answers. He selected his disciples from among the illiterate fishermen of Galilee, and promised them no reward in this world but a part in the bitter cup of his suffering. He dined with publicans and sinners, and mingled with the common people, without ever condescending to their low manners and habits. He was so poor that he had no place on which to rest his head. He depended for the supply of his modest wants on the voluntary contributions of a few pious followers, and the purse was in the hands of a thief and a traitor. Nor had he learning, art, or eloquence, in the usual sense of the term, nor any other kind of power by which great men arrest the attention and secure the admiration of the world. The writers of Greece and Rome were ignorant even of his existence until, several years after the crucifixion, the effects of his mission in the steady growth of the sect of his followers forced from them some contemptuous notice, and then roused them to opposition.

And yet this Jesus of Nazareth, without money and arms, conquered more millions than Alexander, Cesar, Mohammed, and Napoleon; without science and learning, he shed more light on things human and divine than all philosophers and scholars combined; without the eloquence of schools, he spoke words of life such as never were spoken before or since, and produced effects which lie beyond the reach of orator or poet; without writing a single line, he has set more pens in motion, and furnished themes for more sermons, orations, discussions, learned volumes, works of art, and sweet songs of praise, than the whole army of great men of ancient and modern times. Born in a manger, and crucified as a malefactor, he now controls the destinies of the civilized world, and rules a spiritual empire which embraces one third of the inhabitants of the globe. There never was in this world a life so unpretending, modest, and lowly in its outward form and condition, and yet producing such extraordinary effects upon all ages, nations, and classes of men. The annals of history produce no other example of such complete and astounding success in spite of the absence of those material, social, literary, and artistic powers and influences which are indispensable to success for a mere man. Christ stands also, in this respect, solitary and alone among all the heroes of history, and presents to us an insolvable problem, unless we admit him to be the eternal Son of God.

We will now attempt to describe his personal, or moral and religious character, as it appears on the record of his public life, and then examine his own testimony of himself as giving us the only rational solution of this mighty problem.

The first impression which we receive from the life of Jesus is, that of its perfect innocency and sinlessness in the midst of a sinful world. He, and he alone, carried the spotless purity of childhood untarnished through his youth and manhood. Hence the lamb and the dove are his appropriate symbols.

He was, indeed, tempted as we are, but he never yielded to temptation. His sinlessness was at first only the *relative* sinlessness of Adam before the fall, which implies the necessity of trial and temptation. But here is the fundamental difference between the first and the second Adam: the first Adam lost his innocence by the abuse of his freedom, and fell by his own act of disobedience into the dire evils of sin; while the second Adam was innocent in the midst of sinners, and maintained his innocence against all and every temptation.

In vain we look through the entire biography of Christ for a single stain, or the slightest shadow, on his moral character. There never lived a more harmless being on earth. He injured no one, he took advantage of no one. He never spoke a wrong word, he never committed a wrong action. He never repented, never asked God for pardon and forgiveness.* He stood in no need of regeneration and conversion, nor even of reform, but simply of the regular harmonious unfolding of his moral power. He exhibited a uniform elevation above the objects, opinions, pleasures, and passions of this world, and disregard to riches, display, fame, and favor of men. The apparent outbreak of passion in the expulsion of the profane traffickers from the temple, is the only instance in the record of his history which might be quoted against his freedom from the faults of humanity. But the very effect which it produced shows that, far from being the outburst of passion, the expulsion was a judicial act of a religious reformer, vindicating, in just and holy zeal, the honor of the Lord of the temple, and that with a dignity and majesty which at once silenced the offenders, though superior in number and physical strength, and

* The petition for forgiveness in the Lord's Prayer, Matt. vi, 12, is no exception, as it was no expression of his individual need in this part, but intended as a model for his disciples.

made them submit to their well-deserved punishment without a murmur, and in awe of the presence of a superhuman power. The cursing of the unfruitful fig-tree can still less be urged, as it evidently was a significant symbolical act foreshadowing the fearful doom of the impenitent Jews in the destruction of Jerusalem.

The perfect innocence of Jesus, however, is based, not only negatively on the absence of any recorded word or act to the contrary, and his absolute exemption from every trace of selfishness and worldliness, but positively also on the unanimous testimony of John the Baptist and the Apostles, who bowed before the majesty of his character in unbounded veneration, and declared him "just," "holy," and "without sin." It is admitted, moreover, by his enemies, the heathen judge Pilate and his wife, representing as it were the Roman law and justice, when they shuddered with apprehension and washed their hands to be clear of innocent blood; by the rude Roman centurion confessing under the cross, in the name of the executioners, that "truly this was the Son of God;" and by Judas himself, the immediate witness of his whole public and private life, exclaiming in despair, "I have betrayed the innocent blood." Even dumb nature responded in mysterious sympathy, and the beclouded heavens above, and the shaking earth beneath, united in paying their unconscious tribute to the divine purity of their dying Lord. It is finally placed beyond all possibility of doubt by his own freedom from any sense of guilt or unworthiness, and by his open and fearless challenge to his bitter enemies, "Which of you convinceth me of sin?" In this question he clearly exempts himself from the common fault and guilt of the race. In the mouth of any other man this question would at once betray either the height of hypocrisy, or a degree of self-deception bordering on madness itself, and would overthrow the very foundation of all human goodness; while from the mouth of Jesus we instinctively receive it as the triumphant self-vindication of one who stood far above the possibility of successful impeachment or founded suspicion. "If Jesus," says Bushnell, "was a sinner, he was conscious of sin, as all sinners are, and therefore was a hypocrite in the whole fabric of his character; realizing so much of divine beauty in it, maintaining the show of such unfaltering harmony and celestial grace, and doing all this with a mind confused and fouled by the affectations acted for true virtues! Such an example of successful hypocrisy would be itself the greatest miracle ever heard of in this world."

Admit once this fact of the perfect sinlessness of Christ, as is done even by divines who are by no means regarded as orthodox,* and you

* As, for instance, Priestley and Channing among the Unitarians, Hase and Schleiermacher among the Neologians, Theodore Parker and Rousseau among the Deists. Renan, indeed, dogmatically denies the sinlessness of Jesus, but he scarcely even attempts to prove his position. When he does so it is by an imputation of motives which are utterly inconsistent with the recorded facts, or by a version of them so distorted as flatly

admit that Christ differed from all other men, not in degree only, but in kind. For although we must repudiate the Pantheistic notion of the necessity of sin, and must maintain that human nature in itself considered is capable of sinlessness ; that it was sinless, in fact, before the fall, and that it will ultimately become sinless again by the redemption of Christ—yet it is equally certain that human nature in its *present* condition is not, and never was, sinless since the fall, except in the single case of Christ ; and that for this very reason Christ's sinlessness can only be explained on the ground of such an extraordinary indwelling of God in him as never took place in any other human being before or after. The entire Christian world, Greek, Latin,

to contradict the narrative given by those whom he admits to have been eye-witnesses. For instance, he declares the resurrection of Lazarus to have been a fraud played off upon the by-standers, in which our Lord was an accessory, if not an accomplice. He offers no proof in support of this extraordinary assertion beyond his own statement that so it was. Arguments (?) such as these neither need nor deserve serious refutation. They stand self-convicted.—Ed. R. T. S.

and Protestant, agree in the scriptural doctrine of the universal depravity of human nature since the apostasy of the first Adam. Even the modern and unscriptural Romish dogma of the freedom of the Virgin Mary from hereditary as well as actual sin, can hardly be quoted as an exception; for this exception is explained in the Papal decision by the assumption of a miraculous interposition of Divine favor, and the reflex influence of the merit of her Son. There is not a single mortal who must not charge himself with some defect or folly, and man's consciousness of sin and unworthiness deepens just in proportion to his self-knowledge and progress in virtue and goodness. There is not a single saint who has not experienced a new birth from above, and an actual conversion from sin to holiness, and who does not feel daily the need of repentance and Divine forgiveness. The very greatest and best of them, as St. Paul and Augustine, have passed through a violent struggle and a radical revolution, and their whole theological system and religious experience rested on the felt antithesis of sin and grace.

But in Christ we have the one solitary and absolute exception to this universal rule—an individual thinking as a man, feeling as a man, speaking, acting, suffering, and dying as a man, surrounded by sinners in every direction, with the keenest sense of sin, and the deepest sympathy with sinners, commencing his public ministry with the call, "Repent, for the kingdom of heaven is at hand;" yet never touched in the least by the contamination of the world, never putting himself in the attitude of a sinner before God, never shedding a tear of repentance, never regretting a single thought, word, or deed, never needing nor asking Divine pardon, and boldly facing all his present and future enemies in the absolute certainty of his spotless purity before God and man.

A sinless Saviour in the midst of a sinful world is an astounding fact indeed, and a miracle in history. But this freedom from the common sin and guilt of the race is after all only the negative side of his character, which rises in magnitude as we contemplate the positive side, namely, his absolute moral and religious perfection.

It is universally admitted, even by Deists and Rationalists, that Christ taught the purest and sublimest system of ethics, which thrown all the moral precepts and maxims of the wisest men of antiquity far into the shade. The sermon on the mount alone is worth intimately more than all that Confucius, Socrates, and Seneca ever said or wrote on duty and virtue. But the difference is still greater if we come to the more difficult task of practice. While the wisest and best of men never live up even to their own imperfect standard of excellency, Christ fully carried out his perfect doctrine in his life and conduct. He is the living incarnation of the ideal standard of virtue and holiness, and universally acknowledged to be the highest model for all that is pure, and good, and noble in the sight of God and man.

We find Christ moving in all the ordinary

and essential relations of life,* as a son, a friend, a citizen, a teacher, at home and in public; we find him among all classes of society, with sinners and saints, with the poor and the wealthy, with the sick and the healthy, with little children, grown men and women, with plain fishermen and learned scribes, with despised publicans and honored members of the Sanhedrim, with friends and foes, with admiring disciples and bitter persecutors, now with an individual as Nicodemus or the woman of Samaria, now in the familiar circle of the twelve, now in the crowds of the people; we find him in all situations, in the synagogue and the temple, at home and on journeys, in villages and the city of Jerusalem, in the desert and on the mountain, along the banks of Jordan and the shores of the Galilean Sea, at the wedding feast and the grave, in Gethsemane, in the judg-

* The relation of husband and father must be excepted, on account of his elevation above all equal partnership, and the universalness of his character and mission, which requires the entire community of the redeemed as His bride, instead of any individual daughter of Eve.

ment-hall, and on Calvary. In all these various relations, conditions, and situations, as they are crowded within the few years of his public ministry, he sustains the same consistent character throughout, without ever exposing himself to censure. He fulfills every duty to God, to man, and to himself, without a single violation of duty, and exhibits an entire conformity to the law, in the spirit as well as the letter. His life is one unbroken service of God in active and passive obedience to his holy will; one grand act of absolute love to God and love to man, of personal self-consecration to the glory of his heavenly Father and the salvation of a fallen race. In the language of the people, who were "beyond measure astonished" at his works, we must say, the more we study his life, "He did all things well." * In a solemn appeal to his heavenly Father in the parting hour, he could proclaim to the world that he

* Mark vii, 37, is to be taken as a general judgment, inferred not only from the concrete case just related, but from all they had heard and seen of Christ.

had glorified him on the earth, and finished the work he gave him to do.

The first feature in this singular perfection of Christ's character which strikes our attention, is the perfect harmony of virtue and piety, of morality and religion, or of love to God and love to man. Every action in him proceeded from supreme love to God, and looked to the temporal and eternal welfare of man. The groundwork of his character was the most intimate and uninterrupted union and communion with his heavenly Father, from whom he derived, to whom he referred, every thing. Already in his twelfth year he found his life-element and delight in the things of his Father. It was his daily food to do the will of him that sent him, and to finish his work. To him he looked in prayer before every important act, and taught his disciples that model prayer, which for simplicity, brevity, comprehensiveness, and suitableness, can never be surpassed. He often retired to a mountain or solitary place for prayer, and spent days and nights in this blessed privilege. But so constant and uniform was his habit of communion with the great Jehovah, that he kept it up amid the multitude, and converted the crowded city into a religious retreat. Even when he exclaimed in indescribable anguish of body and soul, and in vicarious sympathy with the misery of the whole race, "My God, my God, why hast thou forsaken me?" the bond of union was not broken, or even loosened, but simply obscured for a moment, as the sun by a passing cloud, and the enjoyment, not the possession of it, was withdrawn from his feelings; for immediately afterward he commended his soul into the hands of his Father, and triumphantly exclaimed, "It is finished!" So strong and complete was this union of Christ with God at every moment of his life, that he fully realized, for the first time, the ideal of religion, whose object is to bring about such a union, and that he is the personal representative and living embodiment of Christianity as the true and absolute religion. But the piety of Christ was no inactive contemplation, or retiring mysticism and selfish enjoyment, but thoroughly practical, ever active in works of charity, and tending to regenerate and transform the world into the kingdom of God. "He went about doing good." His life is an unbroken series of good works and virtues in active exercise, all proceeding from the same union with God, animated by the same love, and tending to the same end, the glory of God and the happiness of man.

The next feature we would notice, is the completeness and fullness of the moral and religious character of Christ. While all other men represent at best but broken fragments of the idea of goodness and holiness, he exhausts the list of virtues and graces which can be named.

History exhibits to us many examples of commanding and comprehensive geniuses, who stand at the head of their age and nation, and furnish material for the intellectual activity of generations and periods, until they are succeeded by other heroes at a new epoch of development. As rivers generally spring from high mountains, so knowledge and moral power rises, and is continually nourished, from the heights of humanity. Abraham, the father of the faithful; Moses, the lawgiver of the Jewish theocracy; Elijah among the prophets; Peter, Paul, and John among the apostles; Athanasius and Chrysostom among the Greeks; Augustine and Jerome among the Latin fathers; Thomas Aquinas and Duns Scotus among the schoolmen; Leo and Gregory among the popes; Luther and Calvin in the line of Protestant reformers and divines; Socrates, the patriarch of the ancient schools of philosophy; Homer, Dante, Shakspeare and Milton, Goethe and Schiller, in the history of poetry among the respective nations to which they belong; Raphael among painters; Charlemagne, the first and greatest in the long succession of German emperors; Napoleon, towering high above all the generals of his training—may be mentioned as examples of such representative heroes in history. But they who anticipate and concentrate the powers of whole generations never represent universal, but only sectional, humanity; they are identified with a particular people or age, and partake of its errors, superstitions, and failings, almost in the same proportion in which they exhibit their virtues. Moses, though revered by the followers of three religions, was a Jew in views, feelings, habits, and position, as well as by parentage; Socrates never rose above the Greek type of character; Luther was a German to the back-bone, and can only be properly understood as a German; Calvin, though an exile from his native land, remained a Frenchman; and Washington can be to no nation on earth what he is to the American. Their influence may, and does, extend far beyond their respective national horizons, yet they can never furnish a universal model for imitation. We regard them as extraordinary, but fallible and imperfect men, whom it would be very unsafe to follow in every view and line of conduct. Very frequently the failings and vices of great men are in proportion to their virtues and powers, as the tallest bodies cast the longest shadow. Even the Apostles are models of piety and virtue only as far as they reflect the image of their heavenly Master ; and it is only with this qualification that Paul exhorts his spiritual children, "Be ye followers of me, even as I also am of Christ."

What these representative men are to particular ages, or nations, or sects, or particular schools of science or art, Christ was to the human family at large in its relation to God. He, and he alone, is the universal type for universal imitation. Hence he could, without the least impropriety or suspicion of vanity, call upon all men to forsake all things and to follow him. He stands above the limitations of age, school, sect, nation, and race. Although a Jew according to the flesh, there is nothing Jewish about him which is not at the same time of general significance. The particular and national in him is always duly subordinate to the general and human. Still less was he ever identified with a party or sect. He was equally removed from the stiff formalism of the Pharisees, the loose liberalism of the Sadducees, and the inactive mysticism of the Essenes. He rose above all the prejudices, bigotries, and superstitions of his age and people, which exert their power even upon the strongest and otherwise most liberal minds. Witness his freedom in the observance of the Sabbath, by which he offended the scrupulous literalists, while he fulfilled, as the Lord of the Sabbath, the true spirit of the law in its universal and abiding significance; his reply to the disciples when they traced the misfortune of the blind man to a particular sin of the sufferer or his parents; his liberal conduct toward the Samaritans, as contrasted with the inveterate hatred and prejudice of the Jews, including his own disciples; and his charitable judgment of the slaughtered Galileans, whose blood Pilate had mingled with their sacrifices, and the eighteen upon whom the tower in Siloam fell and slew them. "Think ye," he addressed the children of superstition, "that these men were sinners above all the Galileans, and above all men that dwelt in

Jerusalem, because they suffered such things? I tell you, Nay: but, except ye repent, ye shall all likewise perish." All the words and all the actions of Christ, while they were fully adapted to the occasions which called them forth, retain their force and applicability, undiminished, to all ages and nations. He is the same unsurpassed and unsurpassable model of every virtue to the Christians of every generation, every clime, every sect, every nation, and every race.

It must not be supposed, however, that a complete catalogue of virtues would do justice to the character under consideration. It is not only the completeness, but still more the even proportion and perfect harmony of virtues and graces, apparently opposite and contradictory, which distinguishes him specifically from all other men. This feature has struck with singular force all the more eminent writers on the subject. It gives the finish to that beauty of holiness which is the sublimest picture presented to our contemplation.

He was free from all one-sidedness, which constitutes the weakness as well as the strength of the most eminent men. He was not a man of one idea, nor of one virtue, towering above all the rest. The moral forces were so well tempered and moderated by each other that none was unduly prominent, none carried to excess, none alloyed by the kindred failing. Each was checked and completed by the opposite grace. His character never lost its even balance and happy equilibrium, never needed modification or readjustment. It was thoroughly sound, and uniformly consistent from the beginning to the end. We cannot properly attribute to him any one temperament. He combined the vivacity without the levity of the sanguine, the vigor without the violence of the choleric, the seriousness without the austerity of the melancholic, the calmness without the apathy of the phlegmatic, temperaments. He was equally far removed from the excesses of the legalist, the pietist, the ascetic, and the enthusiast. With the strictest obedience to the law, he moved in the element of freedom; with all the fervor of the enthusiast, he was always calm, sober, and self-possessed. Notwithstanding his complete and uniform elevation above the affairs of this world, he freely mingled with society, male and female, dined with publicans and sinners, sat at the wedding feast, shed tears at the sepulcher, delighted in God's nature, admired the beauties of the lilies, and used the occupations of the husbandman for the illustration of the sublimest truths of the kingdom of heaven. His zeal never degenerated into passion or rashness, nor his constancy into obstinacy, nor his benevolence into weakness, nor his tenderness into sentimentality. His unworldliness was free from indifference and unsociability, his dignity from pride and presumption, his affability from undue familiarity, his self-denial from moroseness, his temperance from austerity. He combined childlike innocence with manly strength, all-absorbing devotion to God with untiring interest in the welfare of man, tender love to the sinner with uncompromising severity against sin, commanding dignity with winning humility, fearless courage with wise caution, unyielding firmness with sweet gentleness. He is justly compared with the lion in strength, and with the lamb in meekness. He equally possessed the wisdom of the serpent and the simplicity of the dove.

He brought the sword against every form of wickedness, and the peace which the world cannot give. He was the most effective and yet the least noisy, the most radical and yet the most conservative, calm, and patient, of all reformers. He came to fulfill every letter of the old law, yet he made all things new. The same hand which drove the profane traffickers from the temple was laid in blessing on little children, healed the lepers, and rescued the sinking disciple; the same ear which heard the voice of approbation from heaven, was open to the cries of the women in trouble; the same mouth which pronounced the terrible woe on the hypocrites, and condemned the impure desire and unkind feeling, as well as the open crime, blessed the poor in spirit, announced pardon to the adulteress, and prayed for his murderers; the same eye which beheld the mysteries of God, and penetrated the heart of man, shed tears of compassion over ungrateful Jerusalem, and tears of friendship at the grave of Lazarus. These are, indeed, opposite, yet not contradictory traits of character, as similar to the different manifestations of God's power and goodness in the tempest and the sunshine, in the towering Alps and the lily of the valley, in the boundless ocean and the dew-drop of the morning. They are separated in imperfect men, indeed, but united in Christ, the universal model for all.

Finally, he unites with the active or heroic virtues the passive and gentle, and thus his life and death furnish the highest standard of all true martyrdom.

No character can become complete without trial and suffering, and a noble death is the crowning act of a noble life. Edmund Burke said to Fox in the English Parliament, "Obloquy is a necessary ingredient of all true glory. Calumny and abuse are essential parts of triumph." The ancient Greeks and Romans admired a good man struggling with misfortune, as a sight worthy of the gods. Plato describes the righteous man as one who, without doing any injustice, yet has the appearance of the greatest injustice, and proves his own justice by perseverance against all calumny unto death; yea, he predicts, that if such a righteous man should ever appear, he would be "scourged, tortured, bound, deprived of his sight, and, after having suffered all possible injury, nailed on a post." No wonder that the ancient fathers saw in this remarkable passage an unconscious prophecy of Christ. But how far is this ideal description of the great philosopher from the actual reality as it appeared three hundred years afterward! The great men of this world, who rise even above themselves on inspiring occasions, and boldly face a superior army, are often thrown off their equilibrium in ordinary life, and grow impatient at trifling obstacles. The highest form of passive virtue attained by ancient heathenism, or modern secular heroism, is that stoicism which meets the trials and misfortunes of life in the spirit of haughty contempt and unfeeling indifference, which destroys the sensibilities, and is but another exhibition of selfishness and pride.

Christ has set up a far higher standard by his teaching and example, never known before or since, except in imperfect imitation of him. He has revolutionized moral philosophy, and convinced the world that forgiving love to an enemy, lowliness and humility, gentle patience in suffering, and cheerful submission to the holy will of God, is the crowning excellency of moral greatness. "If thy brother," he says, "trespass against thee seven times in a day, and seven times in a day turn again to thee, saying, I repent; thou shalt forgive him." "Love your enemies, bless them that curse you, do good to them that hate you, and pray for them who despitefully use you and persecute you." This is a sublime maxim truly, but still more sublime is its actual exhibition in his life.

Christ's passive virtue is not confined to the closing scenes of his ministry. As human life is beset at every step by trials, vexations, and hinderances, which should serve the educational purpose of developing its resources and proving its strength, so was Christ's. During the whole state of his humiliation he was "a man of sorrows and acquainted with grief," and had to endure "the contradiction of sinners." He was poor, and suffered hunger and fatigue. He was tempted by the devil. His path was obstructed with apparently insurmountable difficulties from the outset. His words and miracles called forth the bitter hatred of the world, which resulted at last in the bloody counsel of death. The Pharisees and Sadducees forgot their jealousies and quarrels in opposing him. They rejected and perverted his testimony; they laid snares for him by insidious questions; they called him a glutton and a wine-bibber for eating and drinking like other men; a friend of publicans and sinners for his condescending love and mercy; a Sabbath-breaker for doing good on the Sabbath-day: they charged him with madness and blasphemy for asserting his unity with the Father, and derived his miracles from Beelzebub, the prince of devils. The common people, though astonished at his wisdom and mighty works, pointed sneeringly to his low origin; his own country and native town refused him the honor of a prophet. Even his brothers, we are told, did not believe in him, and in their impatient zeal for a temporal kingdom, they found fault with his unostentatious mode of proceeding. His apostles and disciples, with all their profound reverence for his character, and faith in his divine origin and mission as the Messiah of God, yet by their ignorance, their carnal Jewish notions, and their almost habitual misunderstanding of his spiritual discourses, would have constituted a severe trial of patience to a teacher of far less superiority to his pupils.

But how shall we describe his "passion," more properly so called, with which no other suffering can be compared for a moment? Never did any man suffer more innocently, more unjustly, more intensely, than Jesus of Nazareth. Within the narrow limits of a few hours, we have here a tragedy of universal significance, exhibiting every form of human weakness and infernal wickedness, of ingratitude, desertion, injury, and insult, of bodily and mental pain and anguish, culminating in the most ignominious death then known among Jews and Gentiles. The government and the people combined against him who came to save them. His own disciples forsook him; Peter denied him; Judas, under the inspiration of the devil, betrayed him; the rulers of the nation condemned him; the furious mob cried, "Crucify him;" rude soldiers mocked him. He was seized in the night, hurried from tribunal to tribunal, arrayed in a crown of thorns, insulted, smitten, scourged, spit upon, and hung like a criminal and a slave between two robbers and murderers!

How did Christ bear all these little and great trials of life, and the death on the cross? Let us remember, first, that unlike the icy Stoics in their unnatural and repulsive pseudo-virtue, he had the keenest sensibilities and the deepest sympathies with all human grief, which made him even shed tears at the grave of a friend and in the agony of the garden, and provide a refuge for his mother in the last dying hour. But with this truly human tenderness and delicacy of feeling he ever combined an unutterable dignity and majesty, a sublime self-control and imperturbable calmness of mind. There is a grandeur in his deepest sufferings, which forbids a feeling of pity and compassion on our side, as incompatible with admiration and reverence for his character. We feel the force of his word to the women of Jerusalem when they bewailed him on the way to Calvary, "Weep not for me, but weep for yourselves and for your children." We never hear him break out in angry passions and violence, although he was at war with the whole ungodly world. He never murmured, never uttered discontent, displeasure, or resentment. He was never disheartened, discouraged, ruffled, or fretted, but full of unbounded confidence that all was well ordered in the providence of his heavenly Father. Like the sun, he moved serenely above the clouds as they sailed under him. He was ever surrounded by the element of peace, and said in his parting hour, "Peace I leave with you, my peace I give unto you: not as the world giveth give I unto you. Let not your heart be troubled, neither let it be afraid." * He was never what we call unhappy, but full of inward joy, which he bequeathed to his disciples in that sublimest of all prayers, "that they might have my joy fulfilled in themselves."

* The accuracy of this description will be evident to all who candidly read the Gospel narrative. Yet M. Renan speaks of our Lord in the last of his earthly life as "carried away by excitement" and "oppressed by terror and doubt." He even ventures to say, "Did he curse the hard destiny which had denied him the joys conceded to others? Did he regret his too lofty nature? And, victim of his greatness, did he mourn that he had not remained a simple artisan of Nazareth? We know not."—Ed. R. T. S.

With all his severe rebuke to the Pharisees, he never indulged in personalities. He ever returned good for evil. He forgave Peter for his denial, and would have forgiven Judas, if in the exercise of sincere repentance he had sought his pardon. Even while hanging on the cross, he had only the language of pity for the wretches who were driving the nails into his hands and feet, and prayed in their behalf, "Father, forgive them; for they know not what they do." He did not seek or hasten his martyrdom, like many of the early martyrs of the Ignatian type, in their morbid enthusiasm and ambitious humility, but quietly and patiently waited for the hour appointed by the will of his Father. But when it came, with what self-possession and calmness, with what strength and meekness, with what majesty and gentleness, did he pass through its dark and trying scenes! Here every word and act is unutterably significant, from the agony in Gethsemane, when, overwhelmed with the sympathetic sense of the entire guilt of mankind, and in full view of the terrible scenes before him, he prayed that the cup might pass from him, but immediately added, "Not my will, but thine, be done," to the triumphant exclamation on the cross, "It is finished!" Even his dignified silence before the tribunal of his enemies and the furious mob, when "as a lamb dumb before his shearers he opened not his mouth," is more eloquent than any apology, and made Pilate tremble. Who will venture to bring a parallel from the annals of ancient or modern sages, when even a Rousseau confessed, "If Socrates suffered and died like a philosopher, Christ suffered and died like a god?" The passion and crucifixion of Jesus, like his whole character, stands without parallel, solitary and alone in its glory, and will ever continue to be what it has been for these eighteen hundred years, the most sacred theme of meditation, the highest example of suffering virtue, the strongest weapon against sin and Satan, the deepest source of comfort to the noblest and best of men.

Such, then, was Jesus of Nazareth: a true

man in body, soul, and spirit, yet differing from all men; a character absolutely unique and original from tender childhood to ripe manhood, moving in unbroken union with God, overflowing with the purest love to man, free from every sin and error, innocent and holy, teaching and practicing all virtues in perfect harmony, devoted solely and uniformly to the noblest ends, sealing the purest life with the sublimest death, and ever acknowledged since as the one and only perfect model of goodness and holiness. All human greatness loses on closer inspection; but Christ's character grows more and more pure, sacred, and lovely, the better we know him. No biographer, novelist, or artist can be satisfied with any attempt of his to set it forth. It is felt to be infinitely greater than any conception or representation of it by the mind, the tongue, and the pencil of man or angel. We might as well attempt to empty the waters of the boundless sea into a narrow well, or to portray the splendor of the risen sun and the starry heavens with ink. No picture of the Saviour, though drawn by the master hand of a Raphael, or Dürer, or Rubens; no epic, though conceived by the genius of a Dante, or Milton, or Klopstock, can improve on the artless narrative of the Gospel, whose only but all-powerful charm is truth. In this case, certainly, truth is stranger and stronger than fiction, and speaks best for itself without comment, explanation, or eulogy. Here, and here alone, the highest perfection of art falls far short of the historical fact, and fancy finds no room for idealizing the real. For here we have the absolute ideal itself in living reality. It seems to me that this consideration alone should satisfy the reflecting mind that Christ's character, though truly natural and human, must be at the same time supernatural and Divine.

The whole range of history and fiction furnishes no parallel to such a character. There never was any thing even approaching to it before or since, except in faint imitation of his example. It cannot be explained on purely human principles, nor derived from any intellectual and moral forces of the age in which he lived. On the contrary, it stands in marked contrast to the whole surrounding world of Judaism and heathenism, which present to us the dreary picture of internal decay, and which actually crumbled into ruin before the new moral creation of the crucified Jesus of Nazareth. He is the one absolute and unaccountable exception to the universal experience of mankind. He is the great central miracle of the whole Gospel history, and all his miracles are but the natural and necessary manifestations of his miraculous person, performed with the same ease with which we perform our ordinary daily works.

There is but one rational explanation of this sublime mystery, and this is found in Christ's own testimony concerning his superhuman and divine origin. This testimony challenges at once our highest regard and belief, from the absolute veracity which no one ever denied him, or could deny, without destroying at once the very foundation of his universally-conceded moral purity and greatness.

Christ strongly asserts his humanity, and calls himself, in innumerable passages, the Son of man. This expression, while it places him in one view on a common ground with us as flesh of our flesh and bone of our bone, already indicates, at the same time, that he is more than an ordinary individual, not merely *a* son of man, like all other descendants of Adam, but *the* Son of man—the man in the highest sense, the ideal, the universal, the absolute man, the second Adam descended from heaven, the head of a new and superior order of the race, the King of Israel, the Messiah.* The same is the case with the cognate term, "The

*The most superficial reader of the New Testament must have observed that the phrase "Son of man" is used in a special and peculiar sense. What that sense is, has been fully discussed by many of the most eminent Biblical and Oriental scholars. It marks out Jesus as the model representative man, and, as adopted from the words of Daniel, (Daniel vii, 13, 14, etc.,) is employed as a title of the Messiah. M. Renan, without venturing absolutely to deny this sense of the word, endeavors to weaken its force by telling us that in the Semitic

Son of David," which is frequently given to Christ, as by the blind men, the Syrophenician woman, and the people at large. The appellation does not express, as many suppose, the humiliation and condescension of Christ simply, but rather his elevation above the ordinary level, and the actualization in him and through him of the ideal standard of human nature under its moral and religious aspect, or in its relation to God. This interpretation is suggested grammatically by the use of the definitive article, and historically by the origin of the term in Daniel vii, 13, where it signifies the Messiah as the head of a universal and eternal kingdom. It commends itself, moreover, at once as most natural and significant in such passages as, "Ye shall see heaven open, and the angels

languages it is a simple synonym of *man*. Overlooking its obvious meaning in innumerable other passages, he argues, from John vii, 34, that the Jews did not understand it in any Messianic sense, and insinuates that our Lord used it in an equivocal manner, either as a humble epithet, or as a claim to the Messiahship, as the interests of the moment required.—ED. R. T. S.

of God ascending and descending upon the Son of man." "He that came down from heaven, even the Son of man, which is in heaven." "The Son of man hath power on earth to forgive sins." "The Son of man is Lord also of the Sabbath." "Except ye eat the flesh of the Son of man, and drink his blood, ye have no life in you." "The Son of man cometh in the glory of his Father." "The Son of man is come to save." "The Father hath given him authority to execute judgment also, because he is the Son of man." Even those passages which are quoted for the opposite view, receive in our interpretation a greater force and beauty from the sublime contrast which places the voluntary condescension and humiliation of Christ in the most striking light, as when he says, "Foxes have holes, and birds of the air have nests; but the Son of man hath not where to lay his head;" or, "Whosoever will be chief among you, let him be your servant: even as the Son of man came not to be ministered unto, but to minister, and to give his life a ransom for many." Thus the manhood of Christ, rising far above all ordinary manhood, though freely coming down to its lowest ranks, with the view to their elevation and redemption, is already the portal of his Godhead.

But he calls himself at the same time, as he is most frequently called by his disciples, the Son of God in an equally emphatic sense. He is not merely *a* son of God among others, angels, archangels, princes, and judges, and redeemed men, but *the* Son of God as no other being ever was, is, or can be, all others being sons or children of God only by derivation or adoption, after a new spiritual birth, and in dependence of his absolute and eternal Sonship. He is, as his favorite disciple calls him, the "only begotten" Son, or as the old Catholic theology expresses it, "eternally begotten of the substance of the Father." In this high sense the title is freely given to him by his disciples, without a remonstrance on his part, and by God the Father himself at his baptism and at his transfiguration.

Christ represents himself, moreover, as being not of the world, but sent from God, as having come from God, and as being in heaven while living on earth. He not only announces and proclaims the truth as other messengers of God, but declares himself to be the "Light of the world," "the Way, the Truth, and the Life," "the Resurrection and the Life." "All things," he says, "are delivered unto me of my Father: and no man knoweth the Son, but the Father; neither knoweth any man the Father, save the Son, and he to whomsoever the Son will reveal him." He invites the weary and heavy laden to come to him for rest and peace. He promises life in the highest and deepest sense, even eternal life, to every one who believes in him. He claims and admits himself to be the Christ, or the Messiah of whom Moses and the Prophets of old testify, and the King of Israel. He is the Lawgiver of the new and last dispensation, the Founder of a spiritual kingdom coextensive with the race, and everlasting as eternity itself, the appointed Judge of the quick and the dead, the only Mediator between God and man, the Saviour of the world. He parts from his disciples with those sublime words which alone testify his Divinity: "All power is given unto me in heaven and in earth. Go ye therefore, and teach all nations, baptizing them in the name of the Father, and of the Son, and of the Holy Ghost: teaching them to observe all things whatsoever I have commanded you: and, lo, I am with you alway, even unto the end of the world."

Finally, he claims such a relation to the Father as implies both the equality of substance and the distinction of person, and which, in connection with his declarations concerning the Holy Spirit, leads with logical necessity, as it were, to the doctrine of the Holy Trinity. For this doctrine saves the Divinity of Christ and of the Holy Spirit, without affecting the fundamental truths of the unity of the Godhead, and keeps the proper medium between an abstract and lifeless monotheism and a polytheistic tritheism.

He always distinguishes himself from God the Father, who sent him, whose work he came to fulfill, whose will he obeys, by whose power he performs his miracles, to whom he prays, and with whom he communes as a self-conscious personal being. And so he distinguishes himself with equal clearness from the Holy Spirit, whom he received at his baptism, whom he breathed into his disciples, and whom he promised to send, and did send on them as the other Paraclete, as the Spirit of truth and holiness, with the whole fullness of the accomplished salvation. But he never makes a similar distinction between himself and the Son of God; on the contrary, he identifies himself with the Son of God, and uses this term, as already remarked, in a sense which implies much more than the Jewish conception of the Messiah, and nothing short of the equality of essence or substance. For he claims as the Son a real self-conscious pre-existence before man, and even before the world, consequently also before time, for time was created with the world. "Before

Abraham was," he says, "I am;" significantly using the past in the one, and the present in the other case, to mark the difference between man's temporal and his own eternal mode of existence; and in his intercessory prayer he asks to be clothed again with the glory which he had with the Father before the foundation of the world. He assumes divine names and attributes. As far as consistent with his state of humiliation, he demands and receives Divine honors. He freely and repeatedly exercises the prerogative of pardoning sin in his own name, which the unbelieving scribes and Pharisees, with a logic whose force is irresistible on their premises, looked upon as blasphemous presumption. He familiarly classes himself with the infinite majesty of Jehovah in one common plural, and boldly declares, "He that hath seen me hath seen the Father;" "I and my Father are one." He co-ordinates himself, in the baptismal formula, with the Divine Father and Divine Spirit, and allows himself to be called by Thomas, in the name of all the Apostles, "My Lord and my God."

These are the most astounding and transcendent pretensions ever set up by any being. He, the humblest and lowliest of men, makes them repeatedly and uniformly to the last, in the face of the whole world, even in the darkest hour of suffering. He makes them not in swelling, pompous, ostentatious language, which almost necessarily springs from false pretensions; but in a natural, spontaneous style, with perfect ease, freedom, and composure, as a native prince would speak of the attributes and scenes of royalty at his father's court. He never falters or doubts, never apologizes for them, never enters into an explanation. He sets them forth as self-evident truths, which need only be stated to challenge the belief and submission of mankind.

Now, suppose for a moment a purely human teacher, however great and good—suppose a Moses or Elijah, a John the Baptist, an Apostle Paul or John, not to speak of any father, schoolman, or reformer—to say, "I am the Light of the world;" "I am the Way, the Truth, and the Life;" "I and my Father are one;" and to call upon all men, "Come unto me," "Follow me," that you may find "life" and "peace," which you cannot find anywhere else; would it not create a universal feeling of pity or indignation? No human being on earth could set up the least of these pretensions without being set down at once as a madman or a blasphemer.

But from the mouth of Christ these colossal pretensions excite neither pity nor indignation, nor even the least feeling of incongruity or impropriety. We read and hear them over and over again without surprise. They seem perfectly natural and well sustained by a most extraordinary life, and the most extraordinary works. There is no room here for the least suspicion of vanity, pride, or self-deception. For eighteen hundred years these claims have been acknowledged by millions of people of all nations and tongues, of all classes and conditions, of the most learned and mighty as well as the most ignorant and humble, with an instinctive sense of the perfect agreement of what Christ claimed to be with what he really was. Is not this fact most remarkable? Is it not a triumphant vindication of Christ's character, and an irresistible proof of the truth of his pretensions? There is no other solution of the mighty problem within the reach of human learning and ingenuity.

Let us briefly review, in conclusion, the various attempts of Unitarians and unbelievers to account for the character of Christ without admitting his Divinity.

The semi-infidelity of Socinians and Unitarians is singularly inconsistent. Admitting the faultless perfection of Christ's character, and the truthfulness of the Gospel history, and yet denying his Divinity, they must either charge him with such egregious exaggeration and conceit as would overthrow at once the concession of his moral perfection, or they must so weaken and pervert his testimony concerning his relation to God as to violate all the laws of grammar and sound interpretation. Channing, the ablest and noblest representative of American Unitarianism, prefers to avoid the difficulty which he was unable to solve. In his discourse on the Character of Christ, he goes almost as far as any orthodox divine in assigning to him the highest possible purity and excellency as a man; but he stops half way, and passes by in silence those extraordinary claims which are inexplicable on merely human principles. He approaches, however, the very threshold of the true faith in the following remarkable passage, which we have a right to quote against his own system: "I confess," he says, "when I can escape the deadening power of habit, and can receive the full import of such passages as the following, 'Come unto me, all ye that labor and are heavy laden, and I will give you rest;' 'I am come to seek and to save that which was lost;' 'He that confesseth me before men, him will I confess before my Father in heaven;' 'Whosoever shall be ashamed of me before men, of him shall the Son of man be ashamed when he cometh in the glory of the Father, with the holy angels;' 'In my Father's house are many mansions: I go to prepare a place for you;' I say, when I can succeed in realizing the import of such passages, I feel myself listening to a being such as never before and never since spoke in human language. I am awed by the seriousness of greatness which these simple words express; and when I connect this greatness with the proofs of Christ's miracles, which I gave you in a former discourse, I am compelled to exclaim with the Centurion, 'Truly this was the Son of God.'"

But this is not all. We have seen that Christ goes much further than in the passages here quoted; that he forgives sins in his own name, that he asserts pre-existence before Abraham and before the world—not only ideally in the mind of God, for this would not distinguish him from Abraham or any other creature, but in the real sense of self-conscious personal existence—that he claims and receives divine honors and attributes, and calls himself equal with the great Jehovah. How can a being so pure and holy, and withal so humble and lowly, so perfectly free from every trace of enthusiasm and conceit, as Dr. Channing freely and emphatically asserts Christ to have been, lay claim to any thing which he was not in fact? Why then not also go beyond the exclamation of the heathen Centurion, and unite with the confession of Peter and the adoration of the skeptical Thomas, "My Lord and my God?" Unitarianism admits too much for its own conclusions, and is, therefore, driven to the logical alternative of falling back upon an infidel, or of advancing to the orthodox, Christology. Such a man as Channing, who was certainly under the influence of the holy example of Christ, would not hesitate for the choice, as we may infer from his general spirit, and from his last address, delivered at Lenox, Mass., 1842, shortly before his death, where he said: "The doctrine of the Word made flesh shows us God uniting himself intimately with our nature, manifesting himself in a human form, for the very end of making us partakers of his own perfection."

The infidelity of the enemies of Christianity is logically more consistent, though absolutely untenable in the premises. It assumes either imposture, or enthusiasm, or poetical fiction.

The hypothesis of *imposture* is so revolting to moral, as well as common sense, that its mere statement is its condemnation. It has never been seriously carried out, and no scholar of any decency and self-respect would now dare to profess it.* How, in the name of logic and experience, could an impostor, that is, a deceit-

* It was first suggested by the heathen assailants of Christianity, Celsus and Julian the Apostate, then insinuated by French Deists of the Voltairean school, but never raised to the dignity of scientific argument. The only attempt to carry it out, and that a mere fragmentary one, was made by the anonymous "Wolfenbüttel Fragmentist," since known as Hermann Samuel Reimarus, Professor of Oriental Literature in the College at Hamburg, who died in 1786. His "Fragments" were never intended for publication, but only for a few friends. Lessing found them in the library at Wolfenbüttel, and commenced to publish them, without the author's knowledge, in 1774; not, as he said, because he agreed with them, but because he wished to arouse the spirit of investigation. This mode of procedure Semler, the father of German neology, wittily compared to the act of setting a city on fire for the purpose of trying the engines.

ful, selfish, depraved man, have invented and consistently maintained, from beginning to end, the purest and noblest character known in history, with the most perfect air of truth and reality? How could he have conceived, and successfully carried through, in the face of the strongest prejudices of his people and age, a plan of unparalleled beneficence, moral magnitude, and sublimity, and sacrificed his own life for it? The difficulty is not lessened by shifting the charge of fraud from Christ upon the Apostles and Evangelists, who were any thing but designing hypocrites and deceivers, and who leave upon every unsophisticated reader the impression of an artless simplicity and honesty rarely equaled, and never surpassed, by any writer, learned or unlearned, of ancient or modern times. What imaginable motive could have induced them to engage in such a wicked scheme, when they knew that the whole world would persecute them even to death? How could they have formed, and successfully sustained, a conspiracy for such a purpose, without ever falling out, or betraying themselves by some inconsistent word or act? And who can believe that the Christian Church, now embracing nearly the whole civilized world, should, for these eighteen hundred years, have been duped and fooled by a Galilean carpenter, or a dozen illiterate fishermen? Verily this lowest form of Rationalism is the grossest insult to reason and sense, and to the dignity of human nature.

The hypothesis of *enthusiasm*, or self-deception, though less disreputable, is equally unreasonable in view of the uniform clearness, calmness, and self-possession, humility, dignity, and patience of Christ—qualities the very opposite to those which characterize an enthusiast. We might imagine a Jew of that age to have fancied himself the Messiah and the Son of God, but instead of opposing all the popular notions, and discouraging all the temporal hopes of his countrymen, he would, like Barcocheba of a later date, have headed a rebellion against the hated tyranny of the Romans, and endeavored to establish a temporal kingdom. Enthusiasm, which in this case must have bordered on madness itself, instead of calmly and patiently bearing the malignant opposition of the leaders of the nation, would have broken out in violent passion and precipitate action. "The charge," says Dr. Channing, "of an extravagant, self-deluding enthusiasm, is the last to be fastened on Jesus. Where can we find the traces of it in his history? Do we detect them in the calm authority of his precepts; in the mild, practical, and beneficent spirit of his religion; in the unlabored simplicity of the language with which he unfolds his high powers, and the sublime truths of religion; or in the good sense, the knowledge of human nature, which he always discovers in his estimate and treatment of the different classes of men with whom he acted? Do we discover this enthusiasm in the singular fact, that while he claimed power in the future world, and always turned men's minds to heaven, he never indulged his own imagination, or stimulated that of his disciples, by giving vivid pictures, or any minute description, of that unseen state? The truth is, that, remarkable as was the character of Jesus, it was distinguished by nothing more than by calmness and self-possession. This trait pervades his other excellences. How calm was his piety! Point me, if you can, to one vehement, passionate expression of his religious feelings. Does the Lord's Prayer breathe a feverish enthusiasm? . . . His benevolence, too, though singularly earnest and deep, was composed and serene. He never lost the possession of himself in his sympathy with others; was never hurried into the impatient and rash enterprises of an enthusiastic philanthropy; but did good with the tranquillity and constancy which mark the providence of God."

But the champions of this theory may admit all this, and yet fasten *delusion* upon the disciples of Christ, who were so dazzled by his character, words, and works, that they mistook an extraordinary man for a divine being, and extraordinary cures for supernatural miracles. This is the view of the older German Rationalism, and forms a parallel to the heathen rationalism of Euhemerus, of the Cyrenaic school, who explained the gods of the Greek mythology as human sages, heroes, kings, and tyrants, whose superior knowledge or great deeds secured them divine honors, or the hero-worship of posterity. It was fully developed, with a considerable degree of patient learning and argument, by the late Professor H. E. G. Paulus. He takes the Gospel history as actual history ; but by a critical separation of what he calls *fact* from what he calls the *judgment* of the actor or narrator, he explains it exclusively from natural causes, and thus brings it down to the level of every-day events. This "natural" interpretation, however, turns out to be most unnatural, and commits innumerable sins against the laws of hermeneutics, and against common sense itself. To prove this, it is only necessary to give some specimens from the exegeses of Paulus and his school. The glory of the Lord which, in the night of his birth, shone around the shepherds of Jerusalem, was simply an *ignis fatuus*, or a meteor; the miracle at Christ's baptism may be easily reduced to thunder and lightning, and a sudden disappearance of the clouds; the tempter in the wilderness was a cunning Pharisee, and only mistaken by the Evangelists for the devil, who does not exist except in the imagination of the superstitious; the supposed miraculous cures of the Saviour turn out on closer examination to be simply deeds either of philanthropy, or medical skill, or good luck; the changing of water into wine was an innocent and benevolent wedding joke, and the delusion of the company must be charged on the twilight, not upon Christ; the daughter of Jairus, the youth of Nain, Lazarus, and Jesus himself, were raised not from real death, but simply from a trance or swoon; and the ascension of the Lord is nothing more than his sudden disappearance behind a cloud, that accidentally intervened between him and his disciples! And yet these very Evangelists, who must have been destitute of the most ordinary talent of observation, and even of common sense, have contrived to paint a character, and to write a story, which in sublimity, grandeur, and interest, throws the productions of the proudest historians into the shade, and has exerted an irresistible charm upon Christendom for these eighteen hundred years! No wonder that those absurdities of a misguided learning and ingenuity hardly survived their authors.* It is a decided merit of Strauss, that he has thoroughly refuted the work of his predecessor, and given it the death-blow. But his own theory has shared no better fate.

The last hypothesis, of a *poetical fiction*, was

* The "Vie de Jesus" has appeared since this essay was written. It is strange that the defunct and obsolete theories of the German Naturalistic Rationalists should be revived by M. Renan, and treated as novelties. The absurd attempts of Paulus and his companions to explain away the miracles by natural causes have been standing jokes in Germany for the last fifty years, even among the infidels themselves. These attempts, however, are reproduced, and even carried to a more extravagant length, by M. Renan.—Ed. R. T. S.

matured and carried out, with a high degree of ability and ingenuity, by the speculative or pantheistic rationalism of Strauss. This writer sinks the Gospel history, as to its origin and reality, substantially to a par with the ancient mythologies of Greece and Rome. Without denying altogether the historical existence of Jesus, and admitting him to have been a religious genius of the first magnitude, he yet, from pantheistic premises, and by a cold process of hypercritical dissection of the apparently contradictory accounts of the witnesses, resolves all the supernatural and miraculous elements of his person and history into myths, or imaginary representations of religious ideas in the form of facts, which were honestly believed by the authors to have actually occurred. The ideas symbolized in these facts are declared to be true in the abstract, or as applied to humanity as a whole, but denied as false in the concrete, or in their application to an individual. The authorship of the evangelical myths is ascribed to the primitive Christian society, pregnant with Jewish Messianic hopes, and kindled to hero-worship by the appearance of the extraordinary person of Jesus of Nazareth, whom they took to be the promised Messiah. But this theory is likewise surrounded by insurmountable difficulties. Who ever heard of a poem unconsciously produced by a mixed multitude, and honestly mistaken by them all for actual history? How could the five hundred persons to whom the risen Saviour is said to have appeared, dream the same dreams at the same time, and then believe it as a veritable fact, at the risk of their lives? How could a man like St. Paul submit his strong and clear mind, and devote all the energies of his noble life, to a poetical fiction of the very sect whom he once persecuted unto death? How could such an illusion stand the combined hostility of the Jewish and heathen world, and the searching criticism of an age of high civilization, and even of incredulity and skepticism? How strange that unlettered and unskilled fishermen, and not the philosophers and poets of classic Greece and Rome, should have composed such a grand poem, and painted a character to whom Strauss himself is forced to assign the very first rank among all the religious geniuses and founders of religion! The poets must, in this case, have been superior to the hero; and yet the hero is admitted to be the purest and greatest man that ever lived! Where are the traces of a fervid imagination and poetic art in the Gospel history? Is it not, on the contrary, remarkably free from all rhetorical and poetical ornament, from every admixture of subjective notions and feelings, even from the expression of sympathy, admiration, and praise? The writers evidently felt that the story speaks best for itself, and would not be improved by the art and skill of man. Their discrepancies, which at best do not in the least affect the picture of Christ's character, but only the subordinate details of his history, prove the absence of conspiracy, attest the honesty of their intention, and confirm the general credibility of their account. Verily the Gospel history, related with such unmistakable honesty and simplicity, by immediate witnesses and their pupils, proclaimed in open daylight from Jerusalem to Rome, believed by thousands of Jews, Greeks, and Romans, sealed with the blood of Apostles, Evangelists, and saints of every grade of society and culture, is better attested by external and internal evidence than any other history. The same negative criticism which Strauss applied to the Gospels would with equal plausibility destroy the strongest chain of evidence before a court of justice, and resolve the life of Socrates, or Charlemagne, or Luther, or Napoleon, into a mythical dream. The secret of the mythical hypothesis is the pantheistic denial of a personal living God, and the *à priori* assumption of the impossibility of a miracle. In its details it is so complicated and artificial that it cannot be made generally intelligible; and in proportion as it is popularized it reverts to the vulgar hypothesis of intentional fraud, from which it professed at starting to shrink back in horror and contempt.

With this last and ablest effort, infidelity seems to have exhausted its scientific resources. It could only repeat itself hereafter. Its different theories have all been tried and found wanting. One has in turn transplanted and refuted the other, even during the life-time of their champions. They explain nothing in the end; on the contrary, they only substitute an unnatural for a supernatural miracle, an inextricable enigma for a revealed mystery. They equally tend to undermine all faith in God's providence in history, and deprive poor and fallen humanity, in a world of sin, temptation, and sorrow, of its only hope and comfort in life and in death.

Dr. Strauss, by far the clearest and strongest of all assailants of the Gospel history, seems to have had a passing feeling of the disastrous tendency of his work of destruction and the awful responsibility he assumed. "The results of our inquiry," he says in the closing chapter of his "Life of Jesus," "have apparently annihilated the greatest and most important part of that which the Christian has been wont to believe concerning his Jesus, have uprooted all the encouragements which he has derived from his faith, and deprived him of all his consolations. The boundless store of truth and life which for eighteen hundred years have been the aliment of humanity, seems irretrievably devastated; the most sublime leveled with the dust, God divested of his grace, man of his dignity, and the tie between heaven and earth broken. Piety turns away with horror from so fearful an act of desecration, and strong in the impregnable self-evidence of its faith, boldly pronounces that, let an audacious criticism attempt what it will, all which the Scriptures declare and the Church believes of Christ will still subsist as eternal truth, nor needs one iota of it to be renounced." Strauss makes, then, an attempt, it is true, at a philosophical reconstruction of what he vainly imagines himself to have annihilated as an historical fact by his sophistical criticism. He professes to admit the abstract truth of the orthodox Christology, or the union of the Divine and human, but perverts it into a purely intellectual and pantheistic meaning. He refuses divine attributes and honors to the glorious Head of the race, but applies them to a decapitated humanity. He thus substitutes, from pantheistic prejudice, a metaphysical abstraction for a living reality, a mere notion for an historical fact, a progress in philosophy and mechanical arts for the moral victory over sin and death, a pantheistic hero-worship or self-adoration of a fallen race for the worship of the only true and living God, the gift of a stone for the bread of eternal life!

Humanity scorns such a miserable substitute, which has yet to give the first proof of any power for good, and which will never convert or improve a single individual. It must have a living head, a real Lord and Saviour from sin and death. With renewed faith and confidence, it returns from the dreary desolations of a heartless infidelity and the vain conceits of a philosophy falsely so called, to the historical Christ, and exclaims with Peter: "Lord, to whom shall we go? thou hast the words of eternal life: and we believe and are sure that thou art that Christ, the Son of the living God."

Yes! there he lives, the Divine man and incarnate God, on the ever fresh and self-authenticating record of the Gospels, in the unbroken history of eighteen centuries, and in the hearts and lives of the wisest and best of our race. Jesus Christ is the most certain, the most sacred, and the most glorious of all facts, arrayed in a beauty and majesty which throws the "starry heavens above us, and the moral law within us," into obscurity, and fills us truly with ever-growing reverence and awe. He shines forth like the self-evidencing light of the noonday sun. He is too great, too pure, too perfect to have been invented by any sinful and erring man. His character and claims are confirmed by the sublimest doctrine, the purest ethics, the mightiest miracles, the grandest spiritual kingdom, and are daily and hourly exhibited in the virtues and graces of all who yield to the regenerating and sanctifying power of his Spirit and example. The historical Christ meets and satisfies our deepest intellectual and moral wants. Our souls, if left to their noblest impulses and aspirations, instinctively turn to him as the needle to the magnet, as the flower to the sun, as the panting hart to the fresh fountain. We are made for him, and "our heart is without rest until it rests in him." He commands our assent, he wins our admiration, he overwhelms us to humble adoration and worship. We cannot look upon him without spiritual benefit. We cannot think of him without being elevated above all that is low and mean, and encouraged to all that is good and noble. The very hem of his garment is healing to the touch; one hour spent in his communion outweighs all the pleasures of sin. He is the most precious and indispensable gift of a merciful God to a fallen world. In him are the treasures of true wisdom, in him the fountain of pardon and peace, in him the only substantial hope and comfort in this world and that which is to come. Without him, history is a dreary waste, an inextricable enigma; with him, it is the unfolding of a plan of infinite wisdom and love. He is the glory of the past, the life of the present, the hope of the future. Mankind could better afford to lose the whole literature of Greece and Rome, of Germany and France, of England and America, than the story of Jesus of Nazareth. Not for all the wealth and wisdom of this world would I weaken the faith of the humblest Christian in his Divine Lord and Saviour; but if, by the grace of God, I could convert a single skeptic to a child-like faith in Him who lived and died for me and for all, I should feel that I had not lived in vain.

THE

ROMANCE OF M. RENAN.

By Napoléon Roussel.

THE

ROMANCE OF M. RENAN.

We have, once more and again, read "The Life of Jesus," by M. Renan. The book is a masterpiece of skill. We say this without any reference either to its style or to its scientific character; but with respect to the marvelous cleverness with which its author colors events and fashions men, in order to bring them before the reader under such an aspect as will conceal their true character. Up to the present time the adversaries of revelation had assailed it with coarse invectives: Christianity was "infamous;" Jesus, "an astronomical symbol;" the Gospel, "a collection of myths." The atrocity of these accusations produced the conviction of their falseness. This has been well understood by M. Renan, and he has protected himself from that danger. He has dropped the character of an accuser in order to affect that of the historian, and it must be admitted that the imitation is successful. The position assumed is cleverly masked: blame is tempered with praise; the hand that strikes falls with so much discretion that one might mistake a blow for a caress. M. Renan has so well drawn up his suit that he seems to have a real interest in the accused, whose condemnation he demands. He knows that in order to gain the jury he must take care not to seem to dictate its verdict.

As for ourselves, we confess we do not possess this skill. At the outset we shall let it be seen where we desire to lead those who may read these pages. We do not aim either at a magical style or a refined criticism, but at simple uprightness, relying upon the force of truth itself.

It is in the Gospels that M. Renan obtains

the documents out of which he composes the life of Jesus, and to this source of information he gives the following testimony: "In conclusion, I admit as authentic the four canonical Gospels. All of them, I think, go as far back as the first century, and belong pretty clearly to the authors to whom they are assigned; but their historical value is very diverse. Matthew evidently deserves by far the highest confidence with respect to the discourses he reports; in these we have the *logia*, the notes taken from the living and clear recollections of the teaching of Jesus." (Page xxxvii.) *

After reading these lines are you not reassured? Has not the author already won your confidence by showing so much impartiality toward the Gospels? Yes, but wait: he will not long delay in limiting, in the most singular manner, the effect of his concessions. He believes in the evangelical narrative, except in its miraculous portions. He has beforehand

* The references throughout are to the original French edition.

thoroughly made up his mind to reject as false every thing which may be found to surpass the limits of ordinary history; that is, he is resolved to see in Jesus nothing more than a mere man. Had M. Renan reached this result after examination we could have understood it; but so far from that, he makes this conclusion his starting-point. Before he opens the Gospels he lays down the axiom that all their miracles must be false. He writes, "We do not say a miracle is impossible: we do say, that hitherto no miracle has been clearly proved. Suppose that to-morrow a worker of miracles should present himself with credentials sufficiently serious to admit of discussion; let him announce himself, for instance, as able to raise a dead man to life; what course would be pursued? A commission would be named, composed of physiologists, physicians, chemists, and adepts in historical criticism. This commission would choose the corpse, assure itself that death was real, fix upon the place in which the experiment should be made, and establish a whole system of necessary precautions, so that there should be no room for doubt. If, under such conditions, a resurrection was performed, a probability almost amounting to certainty would be obtained. Yet, as it must be possible always to repeat an experiment, and as in the region of the miraculous there can be no question of ease or of difficulty, the thaumaturgus would be invited to reproduce his marvelous achievement under different circumstances, on other corpses, and in another scene of action. Should the miracle be always successful, two things would be proved: the first, that supernatural facts take place in the world; the second, that the power to produce them belongs, or is delegated to, certain persons. But who does not see that a miracle was never performed under those conditions?" * (Page lii.)

* Having entered upon this course of investigation, we think M. Renan has given proof of much moderation. He might, logically, have gone much further, and have said, All this being accomplished, still nothing is proved; for one might yet suspect the good faith of the witnesses, and the knowledge of the experimenters, and suppose the thaumaturgus to be a mere clever inventor! If, a century ago, such a one had professed

Do not take the trouble, then, to point out to M. Renan another method of attesting a miracle: he declares to you that he wants none. So be it; but then it must be confessed that it is a strange mode of consulting a book in order to extract a history from it, to lay down the *à priori* principle, that the assertions with which the book is filled are either errors or falsehoods; and, placing one's self before the hero one wishes to portray, to say to him, I consent to see in you every thing except what you pretend

his ability to relate what was taking place at a distance of a thousand leagues, and to amputate the arms and the legs of the spectators without their knowledge, the scientific men of the age might have proclaimed a prodigy; and yet the thaumaturgus had been no more than the inventor of the electric telegraph and the use of chloroform. Why should we not discover the art of raising the dead? Go a step further; suppose (a case in point) that really God gives to day to the disciples of Jesus Christ the power to work miracles; what would this prove to certain minds? Nothing! The miracles would no longer be miracles, that is all. You cannot prevent my doubting. Thus the miracles of the Gospel are not designed to convert the [willfully] unbelieving, but to strengthen the faith of believers. Jesus Christ himself said so in affirming of the brothers of the rich man, "Neither will they be persuaded, though one rose from the dead." (Luke xvi, 31.)

to be. I will record your words and your deeds, but these words and deeds as inspired by the thought which I will attribute to you.

No matter, let us see whether the being who is to emerge from these "inductions" (p. 1) will possess the life-likeness, the naturalness, the truth, which will make us say, Such a man has lived.

In endeavoring to ascertain what constitutes the strength of our author we have arrived at this principle, (just in its proper limits, but erroneous in the extremes to which M. Renan has pushed it): *man is inconsistent;* we may find in him both good and evil, both the false and the true. Expressed in these vague terms, the assertion is not unfounded. But has he who uses the assertion the right to conclude from it that man is in such contradiction with himself that we may expect to find in the same person both crime and virtue, both uprightness and hypocrisy, both wisdom and folly, both candor and cunning? Are there no limits to this medley in the same individual? Then let him refuse to affirm any thing in history, and let him renounce those "inductions" which he has made the basis of his judgments in "The Life of Jesus."

In attributing to his hero this mixed character, has M. Renan confined himself within the limits of probability, even in the estimation of those who see in Jesus no more than a man? or has he exaggerated, and has the portrait he has drawn been thrust beyond the truth? This is what the reader will be able to decide after his perusal of the following exposition:

M. Renan's First Proposition: Jesus was Moral.

Let us for a moment accept M. Renan's conclusion as established, "All the ages will proclaim that among the sons of men there never was a greater than Jesus." (P. 459.)

Granted. See now to what height this Jesus raised his humanity, even according to M. Renan himself: "It is allowable to call Divine this sublime person who, each day, still presides over the destinies of the world: Divine, that is, not in the sense that Jesus had absorbed all the Divine, or had been equal to it, (to employ a scholastic expression,) but in the sense that Jesus is the being who has helped his species to make the greatest step toward the Divine. Humanity in its aggregate presents an assemblage of beings, low, selfish, and superior to the animals in this only, that their selfishness is more rational. But from the midst of this uniform vulgarity, some columns rise toward heaven, attesting a nobler destiny. Jesus is the highest of these columns, which show man whence he came and whither he must tend. In him is condensed all that is good and exalted in our nature." (P. 458.)

What Jesus appears to M. Renan to be, from the documents which, with their goodness and defects, retrace his beautiful life, is still not all that he was in reality. Jesus was greater than his biographers have been able to make him. M. Renan says, "The Evangelists who have bequeathed to us the image of Jesus are so much below him of whom they speak, that they constantly disfigure him, through their not attaining to his altitude. . . . One feels, at every line, that a divinely-beautiful discourse is given to us by reporters who do not understand it, and who substitute their own ideas for those which they but partially apprehend. In a word, the character of Jesus, so far from having been embellished, has been diminished, by his biographers." (P. 450.)

. . . "If religion be the essential element of humanity, through it he [Jesus] has deserved the Divine rank which has been allotted to him. An absolutely new idea—that, namely, of a worship founded upon purity of heart and human brotherhood—effected its entrance into the world through him ; an idea so exalted that the Christian Church could not but fail completely in its intentions on this point, so that even in our days only a few souls are capable of realizing it." (P. 90.)

"Finally, let Jesus be judged by his work: the evangelical system of morals remains as the highest creation of human conscience, the fairest code of a human life, that any moralist ever drew up." (P. 84.) "Jesus was more than the reformer of an antiquated religion: he was the creator of the eternal religion of humanity." (P. 332.)

It would be superfluous to multiply these quotations; what precedes will suffice to show that, according to M. Renan, Jesus was not a religion-maker, but a being whose moral elevation had inspired him with the grandeur of his conceptions. Jesus was not God, but he was as divine as man can be, having even far surpassed the most just, the most moral, the most perfect of men. We, too, believe this; we believe these praises to be sincere; and we are only the more astonished at finding the panegyrist attributing to a being endowed with these divine perfections the human defects we are about to enumerate.

M. Renan's Second Proposition: Jesus was Deluded.

How could it be that this morally perfect being, Jesus, though without a divine mission, yet came to believe himself sent from God? M. Renan will explain it.

In the first place, Jesus believes himself to be in communication with God. (P. 75.) Nothing can be more simple than this. His moral condition authorized the belief. There is not an impassable gulf between this spiritual union with God, and the assertion that one is his child, his son. In a certain sense, then, Jesus was able to believe himself a son of God. (*Ibid.*) From thence, by a gradation of thought which we will not undertake to explain, Jesus arrived at the identification of himself with his Father. This is the first transformation.

Again, Jesus had styled himself "Son of man." This was perfectly legitimate, for, as M. Renan tells us, the phrase *son of man* is, in the Semitic languages, the simple synonym for *man.* But as, according to the interpretation of certain schools, this expression was applied by the Prophet Daniel to the Messiah, it followed that the title " Son of man," which in the thought of Jesus meant no more than merely *man,* was used, though seemingly without his connivance at first, to designate him as the Messiah. Hence, a second transformation no less strange than the first: "Jesus found pleasure in the application of this title to himself." Thus already, through the effect of a simple metaphor, a child of God, like you and me, is transformed into a son in a special sense, into the *only* Son, of God. This usurpation, which would have seemed blasphemy to an ordinary Jew, was accepted without conscientious scruples by this excellent being. Jesus, who believed himself a man ; Jesus, veracious, humble, and moral—simply allowed himself to be styled God ! But we have not yet done with these transformations.

Jesus, having assumed the mission of advancing the kingdom of God on the earth, soon persuaded himself that "heaven, earth, the whole of nature, madness, sickness, and death, were but instruments for his use. In the paroxysm of his heroic determination he believed himself almighty." (P. 118.)

If Jesus, without being almighty, nevertheless believes himself to be so, we cannot be surprised that he thought he could heal the diseased. "Healing was considered to be a sort of moral influence; Jesus, therefore, being conscious of his moral strength, would necessarily believe himself to be specially endowed with the gift of healing. Convinced that the touch of his garment, or the imposition of his hands, did good to the sick, it would have been hard if he had refused to the sufferers a relief which he had it in his power to grant. . . . One species of healing that Jesus oftenest performed was the exorcism, or expulsion, of devils." (P. 261.)

That Jesus, in a sort of pious fever, should have persuaded himself that God would give him a superhuman power, we might possibly understand. But that in his first attempt to exercise this miraculous power he should not have discovered that he was self-deceived—that the paralytic did not walk, that the blind man did not see, that the dead did not leave the tomb; in a word, that his delusive hope, disappointed at every step, should not have disabused him as to his imaginary endowment—surpasses our conceptions. We must remind ourselves of what M. Renan elsewhere tells us: "The madman walks side by side with the inspired man." (P. 77.) "Socrates and Pascal were not exempt from hallucinations." (P. 267.) "The finest things in the world have been performed under feverish excitement. Every great creation entails a disturbance of equilibrium, a state of turmoil, for the being who evolves it from himself." (P. 453.) It is true that this explanation annihilates the Gospel miracles, and makes Jesus mad and infatuated. Such a state of mind badly harmonizes with the moral excellence ascribed to Jesus Christ by our author. And yet there is another which, if possible, agrees with it still less. This we shall now examine.

M. Renan's Third Proposition: Jesus was an Impostor.

M. Renan does not charge Jesus with imposture any more openly than he charges him with hallucination: he is scrupulous as to the terms he uses. He covers over with the gloss of necessity even that which in the conduct of Jesus is ambiguous. In order to excuse Jesus, he attributes to him the old principle of all religion-makers, that we may conscientiously do evil that good may come.

"Merely to conceive what is good," says M. Renan, "is not sufficient: you must insure its success among men. To this end means not absolutely pure are necessary." (P. 92.) "You must demand of humanity the greater, in order to obtain from it the less. The extraordinary moral progress due to the Gospel comes from its exaggerations." (P. 316.) After such a profession of principles on the part of our critic, we must not be surprised that he should apply them to his hero; but, at the risk of appearing ridiculously severe, we shall continue to regard as impossible the entrance of the least duplicity in the acknowledged moral character of Jesus Christ.

We have seen Jesus persuading himself that he possessed a miraculous power which he really had not: it seems that he had not always that persuasion, and that, when necessary, a little skill took its place. Thus, "sometimes," says M. Renan, "Jesus made use of an innocent artifice. [*Innocent* artifice!] He professed to have some secret knowledge respecting a person he wished to gain. Dissembling the true secret of his power, I mean his superiority over that by which he was surrounded, he allowed the belief to satisfy the ideas of the time, that secrets were revealed and hearts opened to him by a revelation from on high." (P. 162.) "Thanks to some fertile mistakes, Jesus, by adopting the Utopias of his age, transformed them into exalted truths." (P. 284.)

"Even during the life-time of Jesus, many charlatans, without being his disciples, cast out devils in his name. . . . Jesus, who saw in this a homage paid to his renown, was not very severe toward them." (P. 295.)

To recapitulate: "Not being severe toward charlatans who were well disposed toward him;" "out of a Utopia to make a truth, thanks to fertile mistakes;" "to allow the belief in a revelation from on high, which revealed secrets to him;" "to dissemble and to use guile"—such are the means used by the sincere Jesus to proclaim the truth and to commend his morality; such are the resources which explain his triumphs, and on which we are to congratulate the Divine founder of the religion of the human race! Further developments would be useless; we shall, therefore, bring this subject to a close by putting before the conscience of the reader this simple question: Does such a being seem to you to rise to the height of the task ascribed to him? Do these opposite traits in his character appear to make a harmonious whole? Have we here such a naturalness of type, that, after having contemplated it, we are forced to say, It has existed? If to-day a fifth Gospel should be discovered, presenting Jesus to us as M. Renan depicts him, should we be compelled to say, "Here is the impress of reality?" And, if it were necessary to attribute this Gospel to a writer of the first centuries, should we fix upon Paul or Porphyry?

No, this is not the Jesus of our Gospels: it is Jesus put a second time into the hands of Herod and Pilate, of the soldiers and the servants; that is, Jesus humiliated, spat upon, and smitten, a Jesus invented. I can understand that the old portrait of *our* Jesus should not please M. Renan: he must repaint it, cover it with his own colors, and disfigure it, that we might learn to despise it. Thus, as he advances, our author treats Jesus with less respect; blames him more freely, and without regret tarnishes his virtues. His morality ceases to be sublime, and becomes "frenzied." (P. 314.) He praises his disciples "for being unworthy sons and bad patriots, provided it be for Christ's sake that they resist their parents and rebel against their country." (P. 314.) Henceforth "this morality, made for a moment of crisis," is blamed "for having become a Utopia which few care to realize. . . . The man, according to the evangelical type, is a dangerous being." (P. 315.) The point is reached at last, when it is fearlessly declared that Jesus "was, if we may so speak, altogether unnaturalized: family ties, love, country, had no longer any meaning for him." (P. 316.) And, lest his touching conduct toward his mother and his disciples, in his last moments, should be put in opposition to this idea, the fact itself is questioned. (P. 422.)

Our author has such a strong wish to accuse Jesus, that he is "inclined to believe he deliberately designed to be put to death." His forebodings—but too true—of the sufferings of his disciples, are changed into a "taste for persecutions and punishments." (P. 316.) He is led through false interpretations to such a fearful degree of enthusiasm that "sometimes one might have said he was mad." (P. 318.) Of this, M. Renan takes as witnesses "his disciples" (p. 318) when he should have said his parents, who did not believe in him. (Pp. 323, 327.) Finally, "his ill-temper at all opposition led him to unaccountable and apparently absurd acts." (P. 319.) "Passion, which was at the basis of his character, drew forth from him the strongest invectives." (P. 325.) And "many of his recommendations to his disciples contain the germ of true fanaticism." (P. 326.) To this day the whole world has agreed with Jesus in his admiration for the widow who put into the treasury the feeble gift of her poverty, rather than for the rich who cast in of their abundance; but now M. Renan discovers here "a carping spirit, which takes pleasure in exalting the poor who give little, and in humbling the rich who give much." As to the idea of proportion, which completely overturns this view, and which gives to the story its real point, it does not even suggest itself to our author.

To this day all have agreed in recognizing the profound humility of Jesus. M. Renan changes all this, and discovers that Jesus "is fond of honors," (p. 374;) in proof of which he adduces the vindication of Mary's act in anointing him for his burial! And while writing these words he does not remember that Jesus washed his disciples' feet; that he styled himself the servant of all; that he refused the crown, repudiated the appellation "good," and was "lowly of heart!"

But the most striking proof of the determination to slander Jesus, is the way in which the story of his death is told. We take no notice of the fact that, blended with the recital of the crucifixion, simple and touching as this is in the Gospels, we have details given us here on the various kinds of this punishment, on the drink of the Roman soldiers, and on "the singular coincidence that Barabbas, the murderer, was also called Jesus," etc. No; though these things tend to lessen both Jesus himself and his glorious conduct during his last hours, we prefer not to see a wrong intention in them. But who can fail to discover hostility in what follows? If we find it said that Jesus uttered the noble words, "Father, forgive them, for they know not what they do," it is "according to a tradition;" "and if they were not on his lips, they were in his heart." "John declares that he was present, standing the whole time at the foot of the cross. We may, with more certainty, affirm that." . . . (P. 422.) How, then, with more certainty? Surely the aim of this is clear.

At the same time that Jesus and his friends are lowered, his adversaries are cautiously vindicated. Thus, however the Evangelist may explain it, Jesus truly pronounced the fatal word, "I will destroy the temple of God, and rebuild it in three days." "From the standpoint of an orthodox Judaism, Jesus was truly a blasphemer, a destroyer of the established worship: thus his crimes were legally punished. (Pp. 396, 397.) One sees that, if the judges did no more than administer the law, their sin was much less serious. As to Iscariot the betrayer, while without denying that "he aided in the arrest of his Master," M. Renan, nevertheless, thinks that "the curses heaped upon him are somewhat unjust. . . . There probably was in the deed he perpetrated more awkwardness than wickedness. . . . But if the foolish covetousness of a few pieces of silver turned the head of poor Judas, he does not seem to have completely lost all moral sense, since, when he saw the consequences of his fault, he repented, [such repentance !] and, it is said, committed suicide." (P. 382.) The indulgent biographer even tries to free "poor" Judas from the charge of suicide by insinuating that his death might have been the work of some Christians. "Possibly," he says, "the fierce hate which raged against him led to acts of violence in which people saw the finger of God." To transform the suicide of Judas into a crime of the Christians—does this reveal nothing?

After having nearly justified Judas, M. Renan also nearly justifies Pilate. He traces the first wrong through a labyrinth of religious intolerance, Spanish kings, and Romish clergy, up to the law of Moses, and he excuses the criminal weakness of the Governor by recalling the clerical cruelty which, later on, did what was just as bad! This forensic ability to put out of sight the crime of one's client by recalling the future wrong doings of the pretended disciples of the victim, deserves attention: it discloses both the wish and the inability of the author to tarnish the image of one so held in universal respect that he must not be openly attacked. But we will not be the judges; we will be content with quoting M. Renan's words: "Seeing the attitude the Romans had taken in Judea, Pilate could scarcely help doing what he did. How many sentences of death prompted by religious intolerance, have constrained the hand of the civil power! The king of Spain, who, in order to please a fanatical clergy, gave up to the flames hundreds of his subjects, was more blameworthy than Pilate, since he was the representative of a power more absolute than that of the Romans at Jerusalem. It is a proof of weakness when, at the instigation of priests, the civil power persecutes and annoys. Let the government without fault in this respect cast the first stone at Pilate. The secular arm, behind which clerical cruelty shelters itself, is not the guilty party. No one is permitted to say that he dreads blood-shedding, when he performs it by the hands of his servants." "Neither Tiberius, then, nor Pilate, condemned Jesus. This was done by the old Jewish party, by the Mosaic law." (Pp. 410, 411.)

Every attentive reader of "The Life of Jesus" will perceive that its author has taken great pains to appear as a simple historian, and not as an adversary. We admit that, so far as art could reach this end, M. Renan has well succeeded; all his words are weighed and balanced; yet it was impossible not to reveal his ideas, and we have seen how this has been done. We do not, in this short review, pretend to discuss historical facts; but we wish simply to signalize the intention which directs the ready and clever pen of the writer, and to prove that it is not so impartial as it is declared to be. We do not complain that M. Renan, or any one else, should say that he does not believe in Jesus Christ; but we could wish for more openness and candor. Possibly we may be judged rather uncouth. At any rate we shall not be accused of having wished to give currency to our thought under the shelter of an apparent indifference. We think it possible to be impartial, while confessing at the same time our confidence in revelation.

In order to reduce Jesus to the stature of an ordinary man it is not sufficient to lessen him, but it is also necessary, by a concurrence of natural circumstances, to explain how he, simple mortal as he was, could raise himself to that work which, even to this day, astonishes the unbelievers themselves. We shall see how M. Renan, in order to reach this result, lays under tribute the times, the country, and the men in whose midst Jesus lived. For the sake both of fidelity and conciseness we shall, with some abbreviations, quote our author:

. . . "No historical scene was so fit as that in which Jesus grew to develop those hidden forces which humanity keeps, as it were, in reserve, and which it does not bring forward except in days of excitement and peril."

. . . "A gigantic dream had, for ages, pursued the Jewish people, perpetually renewing its youth in its decrepitude. . . . Judea had concentrated the whole strength of its love and desire upon the future of its national existence. It had faith in divine promises of a boundless destiny. . . . At the period of the captivity a gifted poet saw the splendor of a future Jerusalem, to which the nations and the distant isles would be tributary, under colors so fair that one might suppose a ray from the looks of Jesus had reached him across a distance of six centuries."

"The victory of Cyrus seemed for some time to realize all that had been hoped from it, . . . but the triumphant and frequently brutal entrance into Asia of the Greek and Roman civilization threw him back upon his dreams. More than ever did he invoke the Messiah as the judge and avenger of the nations."

. . . "If Israel had held the spiritualistic doctrine, so called, which divides man into two parts, the body and the soul, and thinks it quite natural that while the body decays the soul should survive, this paroxysm of rage and energetic protestation would not have occurred. . . . The Pharisees had recourse to the dogma of the resurrection. The just will live again to participate in the Messianic reign. They will return in the body, and to a world of which they will be the kings and judges. . . . The idea of the resurrection, totally different as it is from that of the immortality of the soul, springs very naturally both from the earlier beliefs and the position of the people. Combining with the belief in the Messiah, and with the doctrine of the future restoration of all things, that idea formed the basis of those apocalyptic theories which were hatching in every man's imagination, and which caused an extreme fermentation throughout the Jewish world."

. . . "Jesus, as soon as he began to think, entered into the burning atmosphere created in Palestine by the ideas we have described. Freed from egotism, he had no thought but for his work, his race, and humanity. These mountains, this sea, this azure sky, those lofty plains in the distant horizon, were to him, not the melancholy vision of a soul which interrogates nature on its fate, but the unmistakable symbol, the transparent shadow, of an invisible world and a new heaven."

"He never attached much importance to political events. . . . Perpetual seditions, excited by the zealots of Mosaism, did not cease to disturb Jerusalem. The death of the seditious was certain; but death for the sake of the integrity of the law was sought with avidity. At no time had the law a larger number of impassioned partisans than when *he* began to live who, by the full authority of his mission and of his genius, was about to abrogate it."

. . . "An undertaking which exercised a great influence on Jesus was that of Judas the

Gaulonite, or the Galilean. Judas was, evidently, the chief of a Galilean sect, preoccupied with Messianic aspirations, but attempting at last a political revolution. The Procurator Coponius crushed the sedition of the Gaulonite, but the school survived, and preserved its chiefs. . . . Jesus may have seen this Judas; . . . at any rate he was acquainted with his school, and probably it was in opposition to his error that he pronounced the axiom respecting Cesar's penny. The wise Jesus, far enough from all thought of sedition, profited by the mistake of his predecessor, and dreamed of another kingdom and another deliverance."

. . . "Galilee was a verdant, well-shaded, smiling country, the true land of the Song of Songs, and of the hymns of the well-beloved. During the two months of March and April the country is a thick mass of flowers of an incomparable richness and variety of colors. The animals here are small, but extremely gentle. Turtle-doves, delicate and lively; blue-birds, so light that they scarce bend the grass on which they perch; tufted larks, which place themselves almost under one's feet; small river turtles, with quick, mild eyes; grave and modest-looking storks—all, free from timidity, allow the very near approach of man, and seem to call him to them. In no country of the world do the mountains stretch themselves out with more harmony, or inspire loftier thoughts. Jesus seems to have specially loved them.* The most important scenes of his divine career were on the mountains: it was there he was most inspired; it was there he held secret interviews with the ancient prophets, and that he seemed to the eyes of his disciples as already transfigured."

... "The country was certainly charming: it abounded with cool waters and fruits; the large farms were shaded with vines and fig-trees; the gardens were masses of lemon, pomegranate, and orange trees. The wine was delicious. . . . So quiet and easily satisfied a life . . . spiritualized itself into ethereal dreams,

* Matt. v, 1; xiv, 23; Luke vi, 12.

into a sort of poetic mysticism, blending together both heaven and earth. . . . Why should the friends of the bridegroom fast while the bridegroom was with them? Shall not joy be a part of the kingdom of God? Is she not the daughter of the humble-hearted, and of the men of good-will?"

"The whole history of the rise of Christianity has thus become a sweet pastoral. A Messiah at a marriage-feast; the courtesan and the honest Zaccheus invited to its festivals; the founders of the kingdom of heaven like a bridal-train—this is what Galilee has dared, and what she has made the world accept. . . . Galilee has placed within the region of the popular imagination the most sublime ideal; for behind its idyl moves the fate of humanity, and the light which illuminates the picture is the sun of the kingdom of God."

"Jesus lived and grew in this intoxicating scene." (Chap. iv, *passim.*)

Here, then, we have what lay at the basis of the projects of Jesus: "a gigantic dream" of his nation, falsely believing itself called by God to rule and govern the world. What gives to the doctrine of the sublime reformer its heavenly direction, is the fact that, before his very eyes, a political aspirer fails through taking a different course. And, lastly, that which paves the way for the success of his moral teaching, is the harmony between the fauna and flora of Galilee and the sweet pastoral of a growing Christianity!

Let us take up again these three data.

(1.) "This gigantic dream," of a Messiah who should deliver Israel, like all dreams, probably has its origin in reality. And, indeed, M. Renan tells us that, six centuries prior to the attempt of Jesus to realize this dream, a poet (read *prophet*) had announced it in such terms that one might suppose him to have been "penetrated by a look from Jesus." Elsewhere M. Renan himself translates a passage from this same Isaiah, respecting the future servant of God, thus: "The servant of God grew up as a tender plant, and as a root out of a dry ground: he had no form nor comeliness; he was overwhelmed with disgrace, abandoned by men; all turned away their faces from him: covered with shame, he was set at naught. It was because he had taken upon himself our sufferings and our pains. You might have supposed him smitten of God, touched by his hand. He was wounded for our transgressions, bruised for our iniquities; the chastisement of our peace was upon him, and with his stripes we are healed. All we like sheep had gone astray, and Jehovah laid on him the iniquity of us all. He was oppressed and he was afflicted, yet he opened not his mouth: he was led like a lamb to the slaughter, and as a sheep before her shearers is dumb; so he opened not his mouth. Men looked upon his grave as that of a sinner, and on his death as that of an ungodly man. But, from the moment of his death, he was to see the birth of a numerous posterity, and the interests of Jehovah would prosper in his hand." (Pp. 8, 9.)

On another page of the chapter we are

analyzing (chap. iv) we learn that the Jew, "thanks to a sort of prophetic insight which sometimes made the Semitic marvelously apt at seeing the broad outlines of the future, made history enter into religion;" and the author teaches us that "these ideas ran through the world and reached even Rome, where they inspired a cycle of prophetic poems." In a word, the idea of a Messiah, conceived in the midst of the Jewish people, had spread itself through the world, and M. Renan sees nothing wonderful in this. . . . Jesus lays hold of this opinion, and transforms it into a great fact which, two thousand years later, according to his own prediction, covers the world. This harmony between Isaiah's time and that of Jesus, and between this latter and the long history of the Church, realizing the prophecies both of Isaiah and Jesus, proves nothing: the prediction is realized, but this realization is vain, since all miracles are impossible. Be it so; but let it be admitted that the miracle introduced to us by our author is the greatest of all. A people, in virtue of its "Semitic" origin, is apt to foresee the future! A poet, six hundred years in advance, portrays the Messiah in such a way that at all points the life of Jesus verifies the prediction! During nineteen centuries after the death of this Jesus his word fulfills itself, and that because this extemporized Messiah was fortunate enough to attribute to himself a mission which existed only in a dream! All these things make up a greater miracle than all the prophecies of Isaiah with their Christian explanations.

This specimen gives us an idea of the admirable art of our writer. A general expectation, the result of Jewish prophecies, is spread throughout the world at the very time when Jesus comes and responds to it. To this day this very fact has been accepted as a proof in favor of Christianity. This, M. Renan tells us, is an error, and proves nothing. The Messiah does not respond to a providential expectation, but a chance expectation creates the Messiah, and from the moment that he is credited his success is no longer astonishing! We do not attribute these words to M. Renan, but they contain his thoughts.

(2.) Suppose this granted: we will not dispute this point, but we shall transfer the discussion to the adversary's own ground. If Jesus were so anxious to realize the Jewish expectation, why did he so grossly deceive it by pretending to fulfill the Messianic prophecies in a sense quite other than that anticipated by the Jews? The children of Abraham expect a temporal kingdom, flattering to their pride: the son of Mary offers them a spiritual one, which frustrates their hopes, humbles them by putting them on a level with the other nations, and restrains their passions by demanding holiness. Such a kingdom of God must have been, as indeed it was, supremely distasteful to the Jews; yet, among these very Jews, Jesus preached it and obtained its acceptance. Now, would we know how Jesus was led so to transform the kingdom of heaven as dreamed by Israel? It was by his witnessing the failure of Judas in his ambitious designs. "It was probably as a reaction against his error that he pronounced the axiom about Cesar's penny." Jesus "profited by the fault of his predecessor, and dreamed of another kingdom and another deliverance." (P. 61.)

Is not such a use of words an abuse of them? Is it not putting an image in place of an idea? We can easily understand that an ambitious man, finding that course to be dangerous which at first he had thought easy, should turn aside from it to enter upon a new one on the same ground, and thus satisfy his restless ambition. But can we conceive that, finding the earth occupied, he should turn toward an imaginary heaven? that, no longer able to do his own work, he should devote himself to the work of a God, and specially of a God of whom he falsely alleges that he had intrusted him with a mission? What possible agreement of thought can there be between a Gaulonite who incites insurrections, and a Jesus who forbids the use of the sword, and declares that "his kingdom is not of this world?" No; he who both preached and practiced devotedness even to the giving up of his life; he who had such a love for truth, and such a horror for every exaggeration of language that he put upon the same level the most solemn oath and the simple yea and nay, must have had more unity of character: we cannot listen to one of his words without being filled with confidence in his perfect sincerity. The thought that the conspirator Judas the Gaulonite could react upon the conduct of the author of the Sermon on the Mount, is so loathsome to us that we have not the courage to discuss it.

According to our author, Jesus also modified his ideas of the kingdom of God to suit times and circumstances. (P. 271.) Thus, at one time, he saw nothing in it but "the accession of the poor." "The kingdom of God," says M. Renan, in altering the Master's thoughts, "was: 1st, for children and those who were like them; 2d, for the world's outcasts, victims of the social scorn, which rejects the good but humble man;

3d, for heretics and schismatics, publicans, Samaritans, and Pagans of Tyre and Sidon." (P. 179.)

Put in these terms, we see, as M. Renan truly says, "an appeal to the masses." "It is the doctrine that the poor alone will be saved, and that the kingdom of the poor is at hand." (P. 179.) Let us go further, and say, it is the court paid to the populace in order to bring it over to the side of him who allures it with false promises, that he may make use of it when the proper time shall have come.

Did such a thought enter the mind of Jesus? Still less, even putting out of sight the selfish aims attributed to him, did Jesus ever promise the kingdom of heaven to the poor, simply because they were poor? Never. To suppose it would be to falsify his thought, and what his true thought was, M. Renan himself will help us to discover. Rightly does our critic say, "The prophets had, without ceasing, thundered against the great, and had established an intimate relation, on the one side, between the words rich, impious, violent, wicked; and, on the other, between the words poor, humble, meek, pious." (P. 181.)

Here, then, is the knot of the difficulty: in the language of the Bible "poor" often means "humble," and hence the doctrine of Jesus. The poverty contemplated by the Messiah is not the poverty of silver or of gold; it is the poverty of virtue and of righteousness. Hence the humility of which he speaks is not the sense of material indigence, but the sentiment of the want of moral qualities. The saved man is not he who has felt and confesses his physical misery, but he who has wept over his spiritual wretchedness: in a word, the man who is forgiven is the penitent, not the mendicant.

This interpretation is so simple as to be self-evident. We shall see that it is that of Jesus himself. To this end let us take the examples quoted by M. Renan. We shall begin with the best-known, the parable of the Prodigal Son, in which our author tells us, "the faulty one is presented to us as having a sort of privileged love above him who has always been upright." (P. 186.) We have here two mere assertions, and both of them mistakes. For, *first*, the parable concerns, not "the faulty one," but him who returns, saying, "Father, I have sinned against heaven and before thee, and am no more worthy to be called thy son: make me as one of thy hired servants." That is, the parable brings into prominence repentance as the ground of pardon. And *secondly*, it is a mistake to imagine here a privilege in favor of the guilty and to the exclusion of the innocent; since the father, speaking to the latter, says to him, "Son, thou art ever with me, and all that I have is thine." (Luke xv, 31.) And observe further, that this "innocent one," as M. Renan will have it, reproaches his father for the feast he has made, accuses his brother of vices of which the story tells us nothing, and complains of never having had a kid that he might make merry with his friends!

Take the example of Zaccheus the publican, who runs to meet Jesus, receives him in his house, gives half his fortune to the poor, and offers a fourfold restitution to any one he may have wronged. According to M. Renan, Jesus forgives the wealthy Zaccheus because, "on account of some prejudice, he was unfavorably received by society." (P. 189.) No; Jesus forgives him because he is in such a state of mind as that he is willing both to confess his wrongs and to repair them; because he humbles himself and repents.

"He avowedly preferred," our author goes on to say, "people whose lives were doubtful, and who stood low in the esteem of the orthodox notabilities." Yes, Jesus preferred these persons, not because "their lives were bad," but because they repented of having led such lives; and if he had not the same regard for the "orthodox notabilities," it was because they, in their pride, did not feel the need of conversion. Let us not, then, oppose the sinful life of the one party to the respectability of the other, but rather the faith and trust of the former to the impenitence of the latter.

We are not anxious here to give our readers a lesson in exegesis; we ask to be allowed, therefore, to cut short this subject by the decided affirmation, that Jesus never flattered the poor, never courted the mob; but that he always forgave the repentant, and always stigmatized the vices alike of the small and of the great.*

* Here are some examples of misrepresented evangelical sayings:

Jesus, in his teachings, subordinates the interests of this fleeting life to those of eternity. It is not a question of abandoning earth for heaven, but of making the possession and the use of earthly blessings contribute to the increase of spiritual and moral treasures. What can be wiser or more simple than this? Yet M. Renan boldly affirms that Jesus "often proclaimed that whosoever would find the kingdom of God must purchase it at the cost of all his goods, and that even at that price he is a gainer."

How is that to be bought which Jesus gives freely. And how could the Master who said, "Seek ye first the kingdom of God, and all these things shall be added unto you," demand that we shall sell our earthly goods? Is not this a forcing of words one is anxious not to understand? And does not the paradoxical form of the precepts of Jesus explain the whole? For instance, would we contend that Jesus did actually wish his disciples, when smitten on the right cheek to turn the other also, when he himself, being smitten on the cheek, calmly said,

Finally, among the number of causes which contributed to the success of Jesus, M. Renan

"If I have spoken evil, bear witness of the evil; but if well, why smitest thou me?"

As another specimen, M. Renan tells us that during the first Christian age "property was interdicted," and in a note he justifies his assertion by quoting the following passage: "And the multitude of them that believed were of one heart and of one soul: neither said any of them that aught of the things which he possessed was his own; but they had all things common." (Acts iv, 32.) We ask, Is this an interdiction or a law? Is it not the simple declaration of a fact? Was this fact general and absolute? If common sense did not already reply, we should observe that immediately after, when Ananias and Sapphira put into the hands of the community part of the price of the land they had sold, affirming that it was the entire sum, Peter tells them that they might have kept the land; that even after having sold it they had a right to keep the proceeds, and that their crime was, not that they had kept back part of the money, but that, by saying they had brought the whole, they had "lied unto God."

How, again, can M. Renan take *literally* the precept regarding those "which have made themselves eunuchs for the kingdom of heaven's sake?" (P. 300.) Are not the words which immediately follow, "He that is able to receive it let him receive it," a sufficiently clear intimation that the literal sense must be put aside? Surely it is neither critical acumen nor intellect that is wanting to M. Renan.

Again, when M. Renan affirms that "the cessation of intercourse between the sexes was often considered as a sign and places—what? The climate, the vegetation, the valleys and the mountains of Galilee!

We can very easily understand how our author, on his return from the East, should wish to describe to us the famous places he had visited, and even to invite us to share in the impressions he had there received: his great talents are sufficient to make us desire this for ourselves. But when in serious reflection he

condition of the kingdom of God," would he seriously have us believe that the kingdom of God on earth is meant, when we are distinctly told that "*in the resurrection* they neither marry nor are given in marriage, but are as the angels of God in heaven?" (Matthew xxii, 30.)

Lastly, on the eve of his death, Jesus gives expression to his agony in the expectation of martyrdom, and to his wish that the hour might come, for it must come, to be passed through. This was the shrinking of human nature, which, in the distant prospect of a terrible trial, was anxious to shorten the suspense, since trial could not be avoided. Luke xii, 49 and 50, read without break, will be sufficient to make us understand this. M. Renan prefers to divide the context, and to put into the former part a meaning quite contrary to that of the whole. "His blood," says he, "appears to him as the water of a second baptism wherewith he was to be baptized, and he seemed to be urged by a strange haste to meet that baptism which alone could quench his thirst." (Pp. 316, 317.)

said to himself, I will show the world the causes which inspired in Jesus the doctrines which have renewed the moral universe, how could he summon courage enough to put among the number of these causes the configuration of the country, its wells, its leafy shades, its lake, and its birds? When the question presented itself to him as to what were the affinities by which Jesus could gain acceptance for his precepts among the inhabitants of Galilee, how could he discover them in "an enchanting nature, which helps in the formation of a spirit less austere, less harshly monotheistic, and which impresses upon all the dreams of Galilee an idyllic and charming tone?" How could he characterize the history of infant Christianity as a "sweet pastoral," in order to bring it into harmony with a Galilee which "obtains credit for a Messiah at a wedding feast, the courtesan and the honest Zaccheus invited to his festivals, and the founders of the kingdom of heaven as a bridal train?" Are we to suppose that Jesus frequented worldly feasts? that he invited a harlot to his table?

that his Apostles formed the procession of a bridegroom at a wedding? Do not these two or three traits, awkwardly brought together and misrepresented, unvail the writer's wish to lessen his hero? Was it Jesus who invited the courtesan, or was it his host? Are we not told, on the contrary, that she came unbidden, and not as guilty, but repentant? Is this bridal train of Apostles any thing more than a metaphor? Did Jesus *often* go to marriage feasts? Do not all these efforts to exaggerate and distort the facts betray a hostile intention? And these "mountains which inspired lofty thoughts," and where "Jesus was most inspired;" "this wine, which is so delicious and so much drunk;" "this quiet life, which spiritualized itself into a sort of poetic mysticism, blending earth and heaven"—does not all this disclose the wish to lower the lofty work of Jesus to the level of earthly joys, and to humanize what others have thought Divine? We admit that there is something new and striking in the attempt. With a few of the *litterati* it will succeed; but its very novelty proves how far it is from being natural and true. Its author, who, for the sake of his design, finds Jesus at first so easy and so joyful, will later, for the same sake, discover in him a "harsh and sad feeling of disgust of the world, of extreme abnegation—the characteristic of Christian perfection," and will reproach him because "in his moments of hostility against the most lawful wants of the heart" "he forgot the pleasure there is in living, loving, seeing, and feeling." (P. 313.)

But, of all the helps furnished to Jesus in the foundation of his religion by his age and his country, the most important was the belief of his countrymen in the possibility and even the frequency of miracles. Not only did the people believe in miracles, but they loved them, and would have them. Hear M. Renan: "A miracle is, ordinarily, much more the work of the public, than of him to whom it is ascribed. Had Jesus persistently refused to work miracles, the crowd would have worked them for him.

. . . The miracles of Jesus were a constraint put upon him by his age, a concession forced from him by the necessity of the moment." (P. 268.)

Starting from this supposition, M. Renan strives to reach two results apparently opposed to each other, but in reality both helping to support his theory. We have seen that, according to our author, Jesus was both a virtuous being and an impostor; and it is by means of this hypothesis of the blending of good and evil in the same being that he hopes to gain the approbation of his readers. In attributing to Jesus this inconsistent character, one has the advantage of seeming to be impartial. And besides, is not the want of strict moral consistency at the basis of human nature? The biographer is therefore likely to obtain a favorable hearing when he tells us that "Jesus came out as a worker of miracles only late and unwillingly; that it was with a sort of ill-temper that he performed his miracles, and only after having been pressed to it; and that he performed them in secret, and with a recommendation to keep silence respecting them." *

* We may say in passing, that the line of conduct Jesus pursued when asked to perform a miracle was this: he granted the request of faith, but he refused that of unbelief. A little reflection will show us the excellence of this rule. In fact, Christian faith is not an act of credulity, but of confidence; that is, it springs from a moral disposition. To believe in a God who is good and powerful, and in a Saviour who forgives and bestows eternal life, is already to love that God and that Saviour; and so to request a miracle is really to seek a favor which will augment faith and love, and thus lead to greater obedience. Hence in the Gospel narratives we find that the believers whose requests Jesus grants generally follow and serve him. On the contrary, the unbelievers, in asking for a miracle, reveal their perverseness: all they seek is to perplex him whom they affect to solicit. They have beforehand resolved not to believe. If the favor be granted, they will ascribe it to the devil rather than to God, for the sake of resisting the appeals of him who grants it. This explains why Jesus, in his own neighborhood, could perform no miracles. (Mark vi, 5.) Matthew adds, "Because of their unbelief;" (Matt. xiii, 58;) an explanation with which M. Renan was acquainted, and which he might have given us. This is why Jesus, besought by the Syrophenician woman, at first is silent, then refuses; and when by his delay the great faith of the woman is brought to light, liberally grants what she asks. (Matt. xii, 16.) This, too, explains the command Jesus gives to the sick whom he has healed, to keep silence, while they go directly to the high priest who was to verify the cure. (Matt. vii, 4, etc.) Some-

Further still, it is the friends and the disciples of Jesus who, in their imprudent zeal, and without his connivance, prepare miracles for him. His hand is constrained; innocently enough he comes to weep at the tomb of a friend; all at once he is to be made believe that he has raised his friend; and if he cannot believe it, he is at least to consent to allow it to be believed. . . . But this illustration is worth quoting: we shall be careful in abridging it:

"The friends of Jesus were anxious to have

times this prohibition is explained in the text itself, by the application of a prophecy to the Messiah, who does good without seeking publicity. (Matt. xii, 16–20.) At other times we learn from the context that Jesus, in enjoining silence, wished to avoid the premature persecutions which would have hindered the accomplishment of his task. (Mark viii, 30; Luke ix, 21.) M. Renan may either have ignored or despised these explanations; but how could he, to make his accusation more acceptable, affirm that Jesus refused or delayed his miracles because "of the grossness of their minds," (p. 264,) whereas it was because of the perverseness of "an adulterous, unbelieving, and wicked generation?" (Matt. xii, 39; xvii, 20.) This alteration may be without intention, but certainly it is not without influence on the argument.

a great miracle. . . . Jesus, in despair, and pushed to an extremity, was no longer self-possessed. . . . It seems that Lazarus was sick; and probably Lazarus, still pale with sickness, had himself attired like a dead man, and laid in the family tomb. Martha and Mary came to meet Jesus, . . . and led him to the cave. The emotion Jesus felt at the grave of his friend whom he believed to be dead may have been taken by the attendants for the agitation, the trembling, which accompanied miracles. . . . Jesus . . . wished to see once more him whom he had loved, and on the removal of the stone Lazarus came forth bound with grave-clothes, and his face bound about with a napkin." . . . (Pp. 360–362.)

In thus daring to parody the character of Jesus and of his friends, M. Renan must reckon largely on the ignorance of the evangelical text in his readers. He must be very confident of the sympathies of his admirers, to offer them, as probable, the most absurd and the most revolting of suppositions. Here is a man, (I do not say a God, not even a prophet, but simply a man,) endowed, as M. Renan thinks, with the loftiest soul of which history has preserved the remembrance; so pure, so noble, so holy, that his friends at Bethany loved him even to adoration. And then his friends, who adore him for his holiness, combine together to play a comedy which goes to the extent of profaning the grave, and of feigning a dead man, in order to simulate a resurrection! How becoming all this is for a friend who is serious and ill, and of Jesus, the creator of a moral world! How simple, how natural! How ridiculous, if it were not so sad. To say nothing of the fact that a joke will be made to pass for a miracle, and that the Master will receive the honor of a resurrection, can we conceive a convalescent, still pale with sickness, shrouding himself in grave-clothes, and putting himself in a tomb, there to wait for the divine physician sent to cure him, and who will be very agreeably surprised at seeing Lazarus, whom he believes to be dead, come forth from the sepulcher living? If the best friends of Jesus, if even Jesus himself, had been able to lend themselves to such an infamous masquerade, they would not be worth the trouble of even a refutation.

We agree with M. Renan in thinking that in all ages the masses of the people, and especially the Jewish people in the days of Jesus, have been very credulous. If necessary, we might even allow that the number of miracles attributed to Jesus has been exaggerated by tradition; and, moreover, to complete our hypothetical concession, we may suppose that even the importance of each of these miracles has been magnified; but, after all this, do miracles disappear from the life of Jesus? Can it be forgotten that his life is completely interwoven with them, and that, if we strike out one from every page, ten will still remain on each sheet? that if the two multiplications of the loaves be reduced to one, and the five thousand persons fed to five hundred, there will be enough of miracle left to prove the intervention of God? If it be demanded that all the miraculous should be subtracted from the life of Jesus, we must be prepared to maintain that in a reputation and a success acquired solely by miracles, all is without foundation; that the people who followed Jesus through town and country; that the rulers who opposed him even to death; that his Apostles, stubborn even to the point of giving up their lives in attestation of his wonders; that this whole generation of witnesses, people, rulers, and apostles, acted without motive and without reason. . . . In order to keep within the strict boundaries of fact, we shall have to maintain that all disturbed themselves, disputed, and fought, during their whole life-time, simply because a popular man once spoke a few words on a mountain or at the corner of a street! For, at least, we must agree that this man had neither arms, nor money, nor influence at his service. Friends and foes alike ascribe but two things to him—words and miracles. If the miracles be false, the words only remain; and to these few words are owing the overturning of all Judea! If so, the miracle comes back to us in another form, and one might with truth exclaim, "It is the voice of God, and not of a man!"

Among all the natural explanations of the success of Jesus, in his day, which M. Renan might have given us, there is one which, we think, would have been the best. We shall indicate it.

Of all the pretensions put forth by Jesus, the highest was that of forgiving and saving sinners. We abstain here from claiming for him this divine power. We simply affirm that he professed it; that he once said to a man who came to him in faith, "Thy sins are forgiven;" and that to the Pharisees who blamed him for receiving the visits of disreputable persons he said, "I am not come to call the righteous, but sinners to repentance." "I am come to seek and to save the lost." On the cross he promised Paradise to a thief who confessed his crimes and prayed to him. In the temple court he absolved an accused woman, who, far from justifying herself, was humbly waiting the execution of her sentence. At the institution of the Supper, he declared to his Apostles that his blood was shed for the remission of the sins of many. Many times, while speaking of his sufferings and death, he said that it was for this very purpose he had come. Zaccheus, the prodigal son, the publican, the courtesan in Simon's house, all are great sinners who had been saved, that is to say, forgiven, and entitled to heaven, without any merit or claim: in a word, every-where, and under a thousand forms, we find the remission of sins. Suppose this pardon to have been an illusion, still the offer of it had a powerful influence upon the hearts of those who believed they had it from the lips of a God. This persuasion was sure to result in obedience to precepts, the practice of worship, and the endurance of persecutions; and an eternity granted by Jesus and accepted by his disciples could not but have an influence on the life and the conduct of the faithful. How could M. Renan not perceive this? And, if he saw it, why did he not mention it? Without being obliged to believe in the pardon of sins in virtue of the expiatory death of Christ, the mention of the historic fact would have secured an explanation to the enthusiasm of a whole people for a man who, indeed, wrought no miracles, but promised heaven to the repentant. Must we suppose that M. Renan has been silent respecting every idea of salvation, because he knew it was dear to those whose faith he combats with an apparent indifference? Did he, perhaps, imagine that the most efficacious expedient to ruin this doctrine would be not even to seem to have perceived it in the Gospels?

After having removed miracles from the Gospel, to take salvation away from it also would, indeed, be a sure means of obliterating every trace of Christianity in the world. Vain attempt! There exists in the depths of upright and humble souls so true a need of mercy, that no "Life of Jesus," by M. Renan, Strauss, or any other writer of their school, will succeed in turning away these souls from that source of living waters in the Gospel of salvation at which, to this day, they have quenched their thirst. You may tell them they are mistaken, that miracles are impossible, and that salvation is a Jewish deception; these souls will nevertheless remain firmly attached to Jesus Christ their Saviour. Discuss as much as you will, their reply will be, "We do not know whether or not a transcendental criticism has revealed to you secrets hidden from common mortals; but what we do know is, that whereas once we were blind, now we see; whereas once we were athirst, now we thirst no more; whereas once we were full of unrest and misery, now we are calm and happy."

This reply, excellent as it is, is nevertheless not the one we wish to make: to some readers it may appear inconclusive. We shall attempt, therefore, to give a more explicit account of our own faith. In our own way we shall trace the life of Jesus Christ.

We say with M. Renan, that in order to the satisfaction of our reason, we must have presented to us "a doctrine which shall be *unique* and adopted by the whole of humanity." * But one cannot exact of this universality that it shall be complete from all eternity, especially when the doctrine admitted is supposed to be subject to a perpetual process of development. All that can be reasonably demanded is, that this religion shall reveal itself from the very origin of its history. Now this demand is met. From M. Renan's own avowal, "The Semitic race has the honor of having made the religion of humanity. Far beyond the confines of history, under his tent, uncontaminated by the disorder of a world already corrupt, the Bedouin patriarch (not to say Abraham) prepared the faith of the world. The superiority of this faith consisted in a strong antipathy to the licentious worship of Syria, great ritual simplicity, the

* "Études historiques et religieuses," vii.

complete absence of all temples, and the reduction of idols to mere insignificant teraphim. Among all the tribes of the nomadic Semites, that of the 'Beni-Israel' was already marked out for great destinies. A very ancient law, written on metallic tables and attributed to their great liberator Moses, was even then the code of monotheism, and, compared with the institutions of Egypt and Chaldea, contained powerful germs of social equality and morality." (P. 6.)

It will be seen that our revelation is ancient enough, since it comes from "far beyond the confines of history;" and also that in that remote region it was well protected, since, "intrusted to the care of a Bedouin, it remained superior, on the points of social equality and morality, to any thing in Chaldea and in Egypt." And this religion was so marvelously preserved in the midst of the idolatrous nations, that the same writer could find no better way of describing its influence than by saying, "The desert is monotheistical."* If this phrase explains

* "Études historiques et religieuses," p. 67.

nothing, at least it declares a fact—the surprising existence of a monotheistic race in the midst of a circle of idolatrous nations; and, in spite of daily contact, the strict preservation of this monotheism. Our reason, therefore, for believing that this monotheism is a revelation is, that we find it among the Bedouins from the very commencement of history, and that down to our own days the *élite* of the philosophers have never got beyond it. Abraham, Isaac, and Jacob, without toil, started from the point at which—aided by the Bible—Cousin, Jules Simon, and perhaps Ernest Renan, have at length arrived.

Our religion, tending toward universality, as is needful in order that we might believe in its divinity, having commenced under the tent of a patriarchal family, extended over a whole tribe, and then over a whole people. M. Renan himself tells us this: "The depositaries of the spirit of the nation seem to write under the action of an intense fever. . . . Never had man undertaken the problem of the future and of his destiny with a more desperate courage. . . . Never separating the fate of humanity from that of their inconsiderable race, the Jewish thinkers [say prophets] were the first who occupied themselves with a general theory of the progress of the species. The Jew possesses a sort of prophetic instinct, by which the Semite is sometimes endowed with a marvelous aptness to see the broad outlines of the future." (P. 47.)

Lest we should be deceived by our own wishes, we shall take, among all these prophets, only him who is praised by the adversary of Christ's Divinity; and further, in order not to multiply erroneously these predictions, we shall confine ourselves to the only one M. Renan has quoted and translated. The predicted servant "was overwhelmed with disgrace, abandoned by men, covered with shame. He took upon himself our sufferings and our pains; he was wounded for our transgressions; the chastisement of our peace was upon him, and Jehovah laid on him the iniquity of us all. He was oppressed and he was afflicted, yet he opened not his mouth; he was led like a lamb to the slaughter, and as a sheep before her shearers, so he was dumb. Men looked upon his grave as that of a sinner, and on his death as that of an ungodly man. But from the moment of his death he should see the birth of a numerous posterity, and the interests of Jehovah would prosper in his hand."

Still careful not to go astray, we adhere to our wise critic, and we find that subsequently to these predictions the expectation of a Messiah is spread among both Jews and pagans, reaching even to the very center of Roman civilization, where we meet with "a cycle of prophetic poems." (P. 48.) When this expectation has become general, a man appears who styles himself the Son of God. According to our author, this man performs no miracle, but at least he is the first who proclaims "the God of humanity. . . . Rising boldly above the prejudices of his nation, he establishes God's universal Fatherhood, . . . he founds that true kingdom of God which each man bears in his heart." . . . (P. 78.) "His system of morals is the highest creation of the human conscience, the fairest code of a perfect life that ever moralist drew." (P. 84.) . . . "An absolutely new idea, that of a worship founded upon purity of heart and human brotherhood, effected its entrance into the world through him ; an idea so exalted that the Christian Church could not but fail completely in its intentions on this point, so that, even in our days, only a few souls are capable of realizing it." (P. 90.) "Jesus was more than the reformer of an antiquated religion : he was the creator of the eternal religion of humanity." (P. 332.) This Jesus, still without the aid of miracles, casts into the world a few words which become so many fertile germs, such as, "Render unto Cesar the things which are Cesar's ; and unto God the things which are God's." This, M. Renan says, is an axiom "of the most perfect spirituality and the most wonderful justice, one which has established the separation between the spiritual and the temporal, and has laid the real basis of true liberalism and true civilization." (P. 348.) . . . This Jesus, without performing miracles in Judea during his life-time, after his death achieves the most astonishing of marvels: he regenerates the soul of humanity; just as God created a physical world, so he creates a spiritual world, by his word alone. Understand, not by wonderful cures, not by unheard-of resurrections, but without miracles, without wonders. The fact is admitted, that, by simply articulating a few syllables, Jesus transforms the moral universe; and yet we are not permitted to see in this transformation the proof of his divine mission! He has done what no other founder of religion could do, and in such an admirable way as to put him, beyond comparison, above every other; and yet we are not to deem him truthful! Is it more rational to suppose that he has established morality and civilization by means of a falsehood rather than by sincerity? Let us be allowed to oppose to all this a saying we ourselves have heard from the lips of a man who is held by M. Renan himself to be one of our modern lights. The learned Bunsen, speaking one day upon miracles, said, "There are for me two undeniable miracles: the creation of the universe by God, and the salvation of the world by Jesus Christ." Bunsen's premises are sufficient for me, and I conclude from them, "Like Father, like Son."

Two great facts may be brought forward in opposition to us. The one is, that other religions have enjoyed results no less considerable. The worshipers of Buddha are not less numerous than those of Jesus Christ. We grant this, but we say that the force of our argument lies in the nature of the work accomplished. The work of Christ upon earth is totally different from that of all other founders of religion. It is not *more* moral; it *alone* is moral, it alone leads to true civilization.

The other is, that the Church is full of faults. To this all we have to say is, that Jesus never said that in order to become his it would be sufficient to *call* one's self a Christian. On the contrary, he foresaw that there would be both hypocrites and cowards, and he has left every man free to resist conversion.

Thus, all the efforts made to lessen the origin of Christianity do but succeed in better establishing its divinity. Prove, if possible, that the Gospels are not authentic; that the Scriptures are not inspired; that no miracle ever took place; that Jesus and his Apostles were no more than poor Jews, simple country folk; that they were ignorant of history and of all science, and that they had not the least literary knowledge: let all this be very clearly proved, the triumph of Jesus is thus secured, and our answer will be: This man of the people, though without miracles, has nevertheless changed the world's aspect; he has done so after having predicted it. The transformation is such, that no science and no skill can imitate it, neither can they undo it. Observe that the case is not that he has succeeded better than any other founder of religion; it is, that he *alone* has succeeded. His system of morals, compared with others, is not simply superior to them; it is totally different from them. By the side of the Gospel such precepts as those of Socrates are even immoral; and if we would find something analogous to the New Testament, we must go back to the Old, from whence, after all, it came.* Jesus did not simply compose and preach this morality: he has inoculated the world with it, he has put it into human hearts and into the lives of millions of men during a long succession of ages; and all this without miracle, ancient or modern! If the world becomes civilized, it is in the countries where Jesus is known. If there exist some true sciences and some real virtues, it is among the nations where the Gospel is read. If any people seek to instruct and to civilize the barbarians, that people is Christian. No good is done here below except in those spots where the faith of Jesus has been. We therefore repeat, the better

*M. Renan finds pleasure in repeating that Hillel preceded Jesus. True; but Hillel's inspiration came from the prophets, and thus we must always be sent back to the first source, the Bible.

it is proved that miracles had no place in the commencement of Christianity, the more will the immense, magnificent, unique results obtained without them appear to be Divine. According to a principle laid down by M. Renan, "Facts must be explained by proportionate causes." We say, *these results are above man; their causes therefore go back to God.*

THE

CHRIST OF M. RENAN

AND THE

CHRIST OF THE GOSPELS.

BY NAPOLEON ROUSSEL.

THE

CHRIST OF M. RENAN.

I.

WHICH was Jesus Christ: Man or God?

We cannot ask this question in the present day without at once calling to mind a famous work, "The Life of Jesus," by M. Renan. It is useless, we are told, to attempt to enlighten one's audience by simply reading the Gospels, since, in estimating their worth, we are compelled to remember a book, the novelty of which, if not its value, is attested by a circulation in France of fifteen thousand copies.

We, therefore, hold it for the present to be

impossible to enter upon the study of the life of Jesus Christ without in some way encountering the work of his most modern historian. This is the task before us now.

Our personal knowledge of a writer is not always necessary to enable us to judge of his work. Thus, for example, it is perfectly needless that we should be acquainted with either the morals or the creed of a mathematician in order to appreciate his treatises on algebra and geometry. Such, however, is not the case as regards a philosopher, or even an historian. Here it is evident that the writer's doctrines must influence his decisions. Even unconsciously the author will magnify the men and the systems which are in agreement with himself, while he will very heartily despise the persons who differ from him. To know, then, whether M. Renan is in danger either of abasing or exalting Jesus Christ, it is necessary that we should become acquainted with his philosophical or religious principles. We shall not seek our information, either in the author's life or in his previous works, but exclusively (with the exception of one single reference) in the volume we are studying. Judging only, then, from "The Life of Jesus," what are M. Renan's beliefs?

And, first, does M. Renan believe in God, or not? If he does, what is his God—spirit or matter? a person or a thing? To use familiar terms, is M. Renan a Deist or a Pantheist? He is neither.

What, then, is his God? He tells us elsewhere that the name of his God is, "Our Father, the Abyss." This truly happy term is in itself an exposition of doctrine concerning the Deity; it is a declaration that he who adopts the name sees no more clearly into the idea of a God than one can see into an abyss. M. Renan does not affirm that there is no God, but simply that he does not know him. Is it possible to believe in a God of whom we have no distinct notion? No. The theory of "Our Father, the Abyss," will be powerless in our life: this is all we can say for it.

In the next place, what is M. Renan's idea of man? A single sentence from his book will tell us. At page 2 he says: "Man, as soon as he rose above the animal, became religious." If there was a time when man rose above the animal, there must have been a previous stage in which he was not distinct from it, and at this stage man was simply the first of the animals. Whether he was a monkey or an elephant we do not know, but at least he was a member of the family. Whether we like it or not, we are no more than perfected beasts.

Now, between this Father-Abyss and this man the child of the brute, what religious relationship has been established? It could not have been very clear, since it emanated from a God of darkness; nor very close, since it applied to the descendants of humanized brutes. In fact, we shall see, that in spite of all the clearness and the strength which this principle has acquired during the progress of ages, it is still, according to M. Renan, very obscure and very weak.

This supposed relation between man and God varies strangely according as you consult various philosophers and theologians. Some resolve it into love, others into obedience; some demand from us an entire consecration, others speak of ten commandments, and others again only of two. According to Christians, man must be just, pure, faithful; he must honor God, love his brethren, and have respect for their lives, their goods, and their homes. Were we to admit duties so numerous and so imperative, it would be but too easy to convict M. Renan's morality of great incompleteness; we do not, therefore, propose to examine it on all these points. We shall test it only on one point—a point very simple, very elementary, and absolutely indisputable. This one unassailable point is *veracity*. Ought man to be sincere and truthful, or is he at liberty to weaken the rich wine of truth by mixing it, more or less, with the water of falsehood? Let us listen to M. Renan in a series of confessions which cannot but be truly sincere, since they are made for the benefit of readers whom he believes to be in sympathy with himself.

M. Renan, with the air of a legislating moralist, says, "To enable it to bear its burden, humanity has need of the belief that it does not receive its full reward in this life. The greatest service we can render it is frequently to repeat that it does not live by bread alone." (P. 184.)

Humanity, then, believes in another life. But why? Is it because this belief is true? No; but it is in order that humanity might be enabled to bear its burden. In order, then, to do it service and to encourage it, it would be desirable, not to teach, but to proclaim to it, and "frequently to repeat, that it does not live by bread alone."

This language is clever, and the thought is well concealed: but let us tear away the vail and then we shall read as follows: Without faith in the future, man would not patiently bear his burden; for prudential reasons, therefore, let us persuade him that after the day of this short life there comes a long and blessed morrow. We must convince man of this, not because it is true, but because faith in this dogma will insure the welfare of those whom this life dissatisfies.

Our readers, then, need not be surprised if M. Renan, adversary of Jesus as he is, should nevertheless think it wise to preserve a certain faith in a future world, for he teaches us (p. 237) that there are such things as "innocent deceptions." Besides, he distinctly says, (p. 316,) that "in order to obtain from humanity the less, you must claim from it the greater." He is so firm a believer in the efficacy, and, if we may say so, in the lawfulness of falsehood, that he adds, "the immense moral progress due to the Gospel comes from its exaggerations."

Laying aside the Gospel for the present, let us bear in mind the above profession of faith—an immense moral progress is to be obtained by means of exaggerations. If, therefore, M.

Renan should ever teach morality, he will recommend exaggeration.

The above quotations are not the only ones of the kind to be found in his work. Here, for instance, is another: "It is because of its double meaning that his thought [that of Jesus] has become fruitful." (P. 282.) When, therefore, you are anxious to succeed in morals, use duplicity; M. Renan will insure you success. But possibly we may have wrongly interpreted this "thought" with the "double meaning;" perhaps it is meant that the thought was true in both its aspects. No, for the author adds, "his chimera has not shared the fate of so many besides; . . . it concealed a germ of life, which, introduced into the bosom of humanity, (thanks to its fabulous surroundings,) has borne there some everlasting fruits." (P. 282.)

This double-faced thought, then, was a *chimera*, and this chimera, thanks to its *fabulous surroundings*, has borne some everlasting fruits!

Moralists, philosophers, legislators, do you

wish for a people who shall be perpetually moral, wise, and peaceful? Teach it a chimera enveloped in fable, and M. Renan guarantees your success. In any case, whether you reckon upon this success or not, bear in mind that M. Renan thinks that there are innocent frauds, fertile thoughts with double meanings, and that in order to obtain a little from humanity it is necessary to exact much.

It is not meant, indeed, that all falsehoods are equally efficacious. No; one must know how to choose between them; and the best are those which have their foundation in the prejudices of the age or the nation in which we live. With this caution it is possible to transform a folly into a great truth! Thus, listen: "Jesus, by accepting the Utopias of his time and of his race, could, thanks to some fertile misconceptions, transform them into exalted truths." (P. 284.)

We do not complain that M. Renan should profess to believe that Jesus relied on the Utopias of his age, and that he had recourse to misconceptions. What we wish to point out is, the principle accepted by M. Renan, namely, that great truths were the offspring of these Utopias and misconceptions, and that good was the result of error and falsehood. It is not with Jesus, but with his historian, that, for the moment, we have to do.

We have no wish unduly to prolong the study of his principles in this matter of veracity; nor are we anxious to comment upon them, since our readers may do it for themselves: we, therefore, in concluding on this point, confine ourselves to the quotation of a final passage. Our own thoughts upon it will be indicated by simply italicising.

"In the East," says our author, "there are a thousand evasions and subterfuges between good faith and imposture. . . . Real truth is of very little value to the Easterns: they look at every thing through the media of their ideas, their interests, and their passions.

"History would be impossible if one did not openly admit that sincerity has many degrees.

All great things are achieved by the masses. Now we do not lead them except by lending ourselves to their ideas. The philosopher who, knowing this, nevertheless isolates himself, and retreats within his own nobleness, is highly praiseworthy; but he who takes humanity *with its illusions, and seeks to act both upon and with it, must not be blamed.* . . . It is easy for us, impotent as we are, to call this, falsehood; and, proud of our *timid* honesty, to treat with scorn the heroes who have accepted the battle of life on other terms. *When by our scruples we shall have achieved as much as they did with their falsehoods, we shall have the right to be more severe toward them.*" (Pp. 252, 253.)

It will thus be seen that, in our author's estimation, the success which is achieved justifies the means used. Whosoever accomplishes great things by means of falsehood may claim the indulgence of those who have only done little things by means of truth.

Well, M. Renan—No! At the risk of being

called "rustics," we again say, No! We prefer to be truthful, though without worldly success, than to be triumphant impostors. Our conscience protests against your immoral principles, and we must say so in passing.

We are not concerned with ourselves, however, but with M. Renan and the principles he extols. From all that has preceded we think ourselves warranted in concluding that, according to our author, sincerity and truthfulness are elastic, that we may have more or less of them, and that in the event of success no one has the right to be severe toward the impostor who brings his falsehood to a successful issue.

Who now needs be surprised that M. Renan should ascribe to Jesus the doctrines he himself judges to be good? He is anxious to justify those who have learned in this way to secure their triumphs: to ask for more would be too severe. Besides, Jesus lived in the East. M. Renan does not require of him on behalf of truth a platonic love which he, the author, does not himself profess. Hence we now see in the *Life of Jesus,* as it is imagined and interpreted by M. Renan, the hero contenting himself with the same measure of truth which is to be found in the writer. But let us remember that in this estimate it is M. Renan's picture that we have in that of Jesus. Put in his place, we now see what M. Renan would have said and done.

II.

It must be understood that Jesus, whether we pronounce him to be a God or an impostor, could not fail to be convinced of his own great superiority over his contemporaries. Thus M. Renan supposes that he treated them with a "transcendent scorn," and that he indulged in "subtle railing" at them. For example, when the disciples, carried away by a spirit of revenge, ask their Master to punish those who refuse them hospitality, by calling down upon them fire from heaven, Jesus, grieved at heart, says to them, "Ye know not what manner of spirit ye are of." M. Renan sees in this holy answer nothing but a "refined irony!" Thus a "transcendent scorn," a "subtle raillery," and a "refined sarcasm," mark the tone of this "master of irony" discovered by M. Renan. Can we find in the sacred text, or even in the profane writings of the period, a single word to authorize this estimate? Not a single one! But this "refined irony and railing," and this "transcendent scorn," are fashionable in our day; and the writer, who has taken his degree in these arts, attributes them to his hero. Thus M. Renan says of Jesus, "His exquisite derisions, his mischievous provocations, always pierced to the heart. Masterpieces of fine raillery, his strokes are inscribed in lines of fire on the flesh of the hypocrite. . . . Incomparable strokes, and worthy of a Son of God! A God alone can kill after this fashion. Socrates and Molière only graze the skin: this man sends fire and fury to the very bones." (P. 334.)

Here is a noble superiority of Jesus over Molière! Molière merely grazes the skin, but Jesus kills! Such is the admiration accorded to the Saviour! Such are the praises M. Renan gives his hero! Ah! we may now understand why Jesus, though silent when he was scourged, yet sighed when he received a certain kiss.

If the Jesus invented by M. Renan was a mocker and a railer, one need not be surprised at the discovery that he was vain: wit and vanity are so nearly allied. Thus, according to Renan, he willingly allowed men to give him a qualification which did not belong to him; he even acted a part! His historian informs us that when the title of Messiah, or of Son of David, was given to him, he accepted it with pleasure. (Pp. 238, 132.) If a miracle-monger sought to make capital for himself out of the popular credulity, "Jesus saw in this a homage paid to his own renown, and was not, therefore, too severe." (P. 295.) One day his friends went even so far as to get up the farce of a resurrection, and Jesus consented to play his part in it. (P. 363.)

In order, however, that this assumed character of miracle-worker may be invested with more likelihood, we are told that Jesus took it unwillingly, (p. 264,) and even in spite of himself. (P. 268.) "Sometimes Jesus made use of innocent artifices. . . . He pretended to know some secret respecting the person he wished to gain over to his side. . . . Concealing the real source of his power, he allowed it to be thought . . . . that a revelation from above revealed secrets to him." (P. 162.) "It was by a contradiction that the success of his work was insured." (P. 126.)

Better still, with somewhat of irony, M. Renan makes us feel that if we resolve on being more sincere than Jesus we shall miss the end which he attained. "Let us continue," says he, with the subtlety he ascribes to another, "let us continue to admire the morality of the Gospel; let us suppress from our religious instructions the delusion which was the soul of it; but let us not suppose that the world is to be moved by the simple ideas of individual happiness or morality. The idea of Jesus must be taken as a whole, without those timid suppressions which take away from it precisely that which make it efficacious in the regeneration of humanity." (P. 125.) And so, a delusion regenerated humanity! Let us pass on, however: the above is our author's opinion, and it is perfectly natural that he should have attributed it to his hero.

But may not M. Renan, who approves the use of these flexible laws of truth, and ascribes it to Jesus, have used them himself? May he not have done in his book what Jesus is said to have practiced in his work? May he not himself also have employed this irony, this subtlety, this railing, and this transcendent scorn? We are all the more authorized to believe so, not only because in principle he approves of this supple truth, but also because he avows his determination to make use of it. In his Preface, speaking of the historical documents which may prove not to be in perfect agreement with each other, M. Renan tells us that "they must be gently enticed, so as to bring them together."

(P. lvi.) Here is indeed our critic's great secret: an *enticing* of texts, so that they may be brought to say what he desires.* We shall soon see him at this subterranean work. Will he entice the texts in favor of Jesus, or to his disadvantage? What has preceded may have aroused our suspicions: these suspicions will be confirmed by facts. It is simply natural that a writer who extols Oriental insincerity, and even ascribes it to genius, should make use of it himself against his adversary Jesus Christ.

III.

We all know the story of that poor widow who, lacking the very necessaries of life, never-

* By this method we undertake to make *oui* (*yes*) mean *non* (*no*). Do our readers doubt it? Listen. First of all, it is a simple fact that *oui* and *non* are nearly related: *oui* is a monosyllable, *non* is a monosyllable; *oui* has three letters, *non* has also three letters: *oui* contains an *o*, *non* also contains an *o*. Do not be surprised that *oui* should have a *u*, and *non* an *n*. Do you not see that *u* is only *n* upside down? If there are two *n*'s in *non* (*no*) it is simply the same letter doubled; and if there is an *i* in *oui* (*yes*,) the Greeks will tell you that it must be an iota subscribed. You see then, by "gently enticing" it, *no* (*non*) means *yes* (*oui*.)

theless casts into the treasury the two mites which are all that remain to her; and we all think, with Jesus, that inasmuch as this woman has given all "her living," she has done more than the rich, who, in spite of their large gifts, have only given of their abundance. Well, we are all mistaken; and M. Renan, by his process of "enticement," learns from the narrative that the intention of Jesus was "to extol the poor who gave little, and to humble the rich who gave much." (P. 339.)

Again, we all know the parable of the rich man who, clothed in purple, and living sumptuously every day, leaves Lazarus at his gate to die of sickness and hunger. We have all felt that the lesson to be learned is in the contrast between selfish opulence and resigned poverty. Our able critic has seen neither this selfishness nor this resignation: by "gently enticing" the text he makes it portray, not a bad rich man, but simply a rich man without the badness.*

* In order to a complete analysis too many details are necessary. Our author has the art of sheltering himself behind the

The design of this is, that Jesus may be suspected of loving the poor better than the rich, and therefore suspected of communism by readers who are more or less wealthy.

The Gospels acquaint us with two facts concerning John the Baptist which, if made to be contemporaneous, would be contradictory, but which, if placed under their several dates, harmonize with each other. At the commencement of his ministry the Precursor places himself below Jesus; but toward the close of his life John sends two of his disciples with the question, "Art thou he that should come?" What does M. Renan? He treats them as contemporaneous, and charges the first statement

letter: his real purpose is discovered only in the spirit of his book. Thus, in his exposition of this parable, he says, "He [the rich man] is in hell because he is rich; because he does not give his property to the poor; because he dines well, while others at his gate dine poorly." And, indeed, what great harm is there in dining well, while others starve? Ah! if we were poor we might understand it better. Specially so, if the hard contrast between such luxury and misery, good living and sores, lasted our whole life-time, and if, every day, we were refused the crumbs given in preference to the dogs!

with exaggeration, in order to give the more weight to the second, in which John expresses his doubts respecting Jesus. (P. 202.)

Elsewhere M. Renan is anxious to eliminate from the Gospel the central idea on which the Christian doctrine rests; namely, redemption. For this purpose he examines the texts which bear upon the Lord's Supper, the emblem of his expiatory death. Our author, in the first place, gratuitously supposes that "Jesus was fond of the opportunity afforded at meal-times for taking the lead in light and pleasant conversation. Sharing the same loaf in common was considered as a sort of fellowship. In giving expression to his thought Jesus said to his disciples, I am your food; that is, my flesh is your bread, my blood is your wine. . . . Then he would further say, This is my body; this is my blood." (Pp. 303, 304.)

Is not this an admirable use of texts? First, ordinary meals are supposed; then the bread which is common to all becomes the type of communion; then, as the third supposition,

Jesus is led from this to represent himself as the food of his disciples. Then the word "food," which is introduced in the supper by M. Renan, gives place to the phrases, "This is my body," "This is my blood;" and so, thanks to a series of "enticements," a *unique* fact—the great fact of the Last Supper—is transformed into a common habit Jesus had acquired. It is no more than one of the pleasant dinner parties of which Jesus was so fond! Hence, to make this "enticement" all the more easy, great care is taken to suppress the words, "With desire I have desired to eat this passover with you before I suffer;" and, "My blood, which is shed for you." Is there, then, so much pleasantness in conversing about one's sufferings, and the announcement of one's own death? Yet it is in these very words, "I have desired," that M. Renan sees the proof that "Jesus was fond of these dinner parties!" *

* * * * *

* A passage is here omitted in which Renan is shown to make insinuations against the character of our Lord so offensive

When there can be no question as to the *nature* of the love felt for Jesus—as, for instance, when it is the love of the disciples in general, and not that of a few women in particular—the means are still found of falsifying the truth by a clever trick. It is well known that Jesus offered salvation to the repenting sinner. M. Renan alters this, and says, "This charming doctor forgave every one who loved him." (P. 219.) After having thus parodied a doctrine which leads through repentance to holiness, into a feeling which much resembles egotism, M. Renan reduces the model disciples of Jesus to very nearly the standard of children. "Jesus," he says, "almost confounds the idea of the disciple with that of the child. . . . He who is humble as this little one, is greatest in the kingdom of heaven." (P. 192.) According

and revolting that they cannot be reproduced in English without shocking the feelings of our readers beyond endurance. Well may M. Roussel say: "Let us draw the vail before these horrible insinuations, whose very timidity discloses a dread of wounding the public sentiment, and is a better proof of the hero's holiness than of the historian's moderation."

to the words of Jesus, it is not the child as such, but his humility, which is held up as an example. Has our clever critic found out that humility is *almost* the whole of childhood?

After all these insinuations, Jesus is represented as "making progress in his fanaticism." We, on the contrary, see M. Renan progressing in his recklessness. Gathering strength from the past achievements of his pen, he advances more boldly in his accusations, and he does not hesitate to say, "By detaching man from the earth, his life was shattered. The Christian henceforth is to receive praise for being a bad son and a bad citizen, provided it be for Christ's sake that he resists his parents and opposes his country." (P. 314.) Surely if a mere man, especially if a wicked man, were to demand obedience to his commands to the neglect of the righteous laws of a father or of a monarch, we should refuse it. Does M. Renan forget that Jesus claims to be the only Son of a God who cannot command that which is wrong? or does he maintain that a son or a subject must, *under any circumstances*, obey his father or his king? Was Salome right, then, when in obedience to her mother she asked for the head of John the Baptist? Was Nero's slave right when, by the emperor's orders, he stabbed Agrippina? Is not the moral law within us above that of a father and of a monarch? Is it necessary to violate conscience in order to be a good son or a good citizen? M. Renan dares not say so; but here, as elsewhere, in order to justify his opposition to Jesus, he begins by assuming, without proof, that this Jesus is not the Christ, the Son of God.

M. Renan rejects no means of assault upon the work of Jesus. Anxious to set aside the prediction of the ruin of Jerusalem, he is content to say that Jesus guessed it, forgetting that in his Introduction (p. xvii) he had declared the Gospel of Luke to be posterior to the siege of that city, for the sole reason that the details of the catastrophe are too minute. Thus, at one time the prophecy is correct, but then it is only a guess; while at another time it is a fraud written after the event.

At page 343 we find another contradiction. Jesus seeks misunderstandings, and designedly prolongs them; then, in a note, the author questions the authenticity of the passage. If the passage be not authentic, this search after misunderstandings never took place, and the wiser course in this state of doubtfulness would have been to set aside both the note and the explanation. The able critic, on the contrary, extracts from the whole two accusations: he quotes the passage from the sacred text in order to accuse Jesus of a want of straightforwardness; then he questions the authenticity of the quotation in order to discredit the book from which it is made. Thus a word which may not have been spoken becomes a two-edged sword, striking in turn both Jesus and the Gospels!

We proceed to another piece of skill. Jesus, describing those who in his day had the courage to brave persecution by declaring themselves his disciples, and the strength to conquer their lusts by remaining pure in the midst of the general corruption, calls them violent men; that is, characterized by a spiritual violence used against themselves, thereby conquering the fear of a persecuting world and the passions of a sinful nature.

M. Renan, who is on the alert to catch every expression that may bear a double meaning, pauses at this one. In this moral violence done to one's self he sees a physical violence done to an adversary; and the following are the terms in which he falsifies the meaning of Jesus: "The kingdom of God cannot be conquered without violence; it is by means of crises and upheavings that it must be established." (P. 237.)

Truly; but with this difference, that Jesus speaks of a moral violence done by Christians to themselves, while what is substituted for this is a brutal violence done by the same Christians to their adversaries. It is not one and the same thing to slay one's passions and to kill one's brother!

After having dethroned Jesus, our author is busy with overturning his friends, and, in particular, the Apostle whom Jesus loved. M. Renan thinks that St. John was jealous of Peter, and hated Judas. (P. 381, etc.)

On the other hand, he almost justifies the judges who condemned the Saviour; "for," says he, "the proceedings which the priests resolved to take against Jesus were quite conformable to the established law," (p. 393,) "and from the Jewish point of view Jesus was certainly a blasphemer." (P. 397.) Elsewhere M. Renan excuses Pilate, who, says he, "could hardly help doing what he did." (P. 410.) Finally, O gentleness of criticism! we find pity, even almost to tears, for Judas! He is called "poor Judas!" He is found guilty only of "having had his head turned by the foolish coveting of a few pieces of silver," and the attempt is made to absolve him on the ground of his repentance: "Judas," we are told, "does not seem quite to have lost all moral sense, since . . . he repented." M.

Renan's proof of this is that the guilty man committed suicide! (P. 382.) "Perhaps, too," he adds, "the fearful hatred with which he was looked upon may have led to acts of violence in which the hand of God was seen." (P. 438.) The meaning of this is, that probably Judas was murdered by the Christians! Let it be admitted, then, that a suicide which was not committed cannot prove his repentance. But enough. The multiplication of examples would be irksome: those we have given are sufficient for our purpose.

It must be borne in mind that our aim has not been to analyze M. Renan's book, but simply to judge of what amount of confidence we are warranted to repose in him as our guide in the study of the life of Jesus. At first sight we recognize the author as hostile to his hero, weakening the authority of the Gospels, denying *a priori* Christ's miracles, falsifying texts in order to tarnish his character, praising his adversaries, and at the same time paying him equivocal compliments of little moment, but serving to weaken the blows struck, and to prevent the martyr's friends from crying out.

Every one may now judge for himself whether this guide suits him or not. For ourselves, what we have seen of him is enough, and we prefer to walk alone rather than to give our hand to him who wishes to lead us astray.

THE

CHRIST OF THE GOSPELS.

IN beginning the study of the life of Jesus we asked ourselves if we should take M. Renan for our guide: we have seen what amount of confidence his work is entitled to receive.

Whom, then, shall we follow, if we forsake so learned a guide? No one. We will go at once to the source, to the Gospels themselves, for it is there that all commentators are finally constrained to return. We will consult the books written by the immediate disciples of the Lord; first, to ascertain what were their Master's moral principles, and how he practiced them; and then we will proceed with the examination both of the precepts and the conduct of Jesus in the matter of truthfulness.

What, then, are the moral principles of Jesus Christ? And first, what are his principles on the subject of veracity? Is man, in this matter, entitled to the use of different weights and measures, according as he lives in the East or in the West? Is he at liberty to regulate himself by the rule of honesty adopted by his race and the age in which he lives? Does Jesus know any thing of the theory of Oriental sincerity? Does he admit that the end justifies the means? Will he say, with M. Renan, "There exists no broad foundation which is not laid in legends. The only guilty party is the humanity which desires to be deceived?" Will he allow the concealments and the mental reservations which are sanctioned by that too notorious society which bears too beautiful a name?* In a word, will Jesus authorize divers sorts of truthfulness, divers kinds of convenient affirmations? No.

* The Jesuits.

Jesus has but one word for all. His rule is admirably simple; it is a golden rule, a divine rule, a rule we may challenge all the philosophers to surpass or even to equal: "Let your communication be, Yea, yea; Nay, nay: for whatsoever is more than these cometh of evil." Noble and impressive maxim, which bears in itself the seal of its divinity!

But did Jesus obey this precept of perfect integrity? Yes; always and every-where. Follow him from Jerusalem to Gethsemane, and from Gethsemane to the Sanhedrim, you will find him perfectly calm and truthful. Whether it be necessary to assert his divine mission or to brave a danger, he does both with the same simplicity. "Who is the Son of God, that I might believe on him?" asks the man born blind. "It is he that talketh with thee," answers Jesus. The soldiers search for him in the garden, that they may take him before the tribunal: he comes to meet them, and says, "I am he." "Art thou the Son of God?" ask the priests who seek to crucify him. "You have said," he replies, "I am." "Art thou a king, then?" asks Pilate. Again Jesus replies, "I am." Neither hope nor fear, neither honor nor shame, can alter his word: it is ever his own, "Yea, yea." If there be one conviction stronger than any other forced upon the reader of the Gospels, it is this: when Jesus speaks he has no after-thought; he speaks the truth, the whole truth. Unbelievers may accuse him of prejudice, of ignorance, of provincialism, but never of falsehood; and when an adversary does so he rouses against himself a public opinion which is otherwise very indulgent: a striking proof, this, that there exists in the world the firm conviction that Jesus was incapable of knowingly altering truth.

What conclusion are we to draw from this? Not that Jesus was the Son of God, but that he believed himself to be so. Whatever else may be questioned, his sincerity must not be doubted: he said often, and in many ways, I am the Son of God. Let it be confessed that he believed he spoke the truth. Jesus, then, either was the Son of God or else he was a madman! There is no other alternative. But how are we to reconcile this madness with these calm words, these profound thoughts, these humble sentiments, this pure and holy life? A madman may believe himself to be a god, but can a madman transform a world? Was it possible for a madman to conceive the soundest of moral systems, and specially to live consistently with the principles of this morality? Is it likely that a madman could be so wise as to surpass all mankind in virtue, and that his insanity should only be seen in the name he assumes? No; M. Renan himself has said it: "If the madman walks side by side with the inspired man, it is with this difference, that the madman never succeeds." If, therefore, the success of a moral enterprise be the test of wisdom, who was ever wise as Jesus Christ?

Already we may say, Jesus made it a rule to be absolutely truthful; Jesus was faithful to his precept, as M. Renan is to his: and judging them both on this common basis, we may rightfully add, Jesus, in declaring that he was God's only begotten Son, proclaimed a pure and simple truth.

We are not, however, anxious to conclude. We wish, before we do so, to exhibit the moral doctrines of Jesus on some important points, and then to compare his life with the principles he himself laid down. We shall then be better able to judge whether the word of Christ deserves our belief or not.

Among the rules of conduct taught by Jesus upon earth, we seek those which are peculiarly his own. We say nothing, therefore, about honesty in our social relationships, or purity of morals, or almsgiving, or hospitality. These principles, if not practiced, at least were known before Jesus came into the world. That which we shall point out as an essentially Christian virtue is *humility.* Surely there is no one else who claims to be the inventor of this! Neither in ancient nor in modern times has humility been held to be worthy of much attention, much less worthy of praise. In our natural pride, or, should a less distasteful phrase be preferred, in our human dignity, we have never much appreciated the bliss of self-abasement. Our common tendency is rather to exaggerate our own worth, and to seek our own honor. And we think no one will claim the discovery of humility for any besides Jesus Christ. He alone said to his disciples, "Be humble as this little child. Whosoever will be greatest among you, let him be your servant. God exalts the humble, and abases the proud."

This is the first moral principle of Jesus. Did he practice it? In proof that he did, although from the Christian point of view it would be allowable, yet we will not instance his obscure birth, the manger at Bethlehem, the workshop at Nazareth, his death on the cross. No: we might be told in reply that Jesus, a mere man, had no choice either with respect to his cradle or his grave. The proof we give we find in the positions he himself chose. He sits at table with the poorest and the most despised of the people; he washes his disciples' feet; he declares himself meek and lowly in heart; he spends his nights in the mountains without troubling himself to procure a place where he may lay his head; he refuses a crown offered to him by the people; and after having refused a throne, he accepts that cross so ignominious for him, but so blessed for the world. When did Jesus cease to be humble—he who always called himself Son of man, who called his followers *little ones,* and who pronounced "blessed" the mourners, the peace-makers, the merciful, and the persecuted?

We insist no longer upon this point, for we do not suppose that any one will refuse to Jesus the glory of a virtue so little coveted! We are, therefore, content to leave this part of the subject by affirming, that he who first established humility in principle admirably illustrated it in practice. We would, nevertheless, say one thing more. Is not this humility, which no one covets for himself, yet desired in children and servants? Who would not be glad if his neighbors, his friends, his fellow-citizens, were humble in their relations to himself? What is the greatest obstacle to peace and order in the world? Is it not that pride, which is more insatiable than hunger and thirst? And should we not esteem it a great blessing if this pride could be extirpated from the bosom of humanity, without doing damage to our individual claims? Yea, doubtless. We approve of humility in a treatise on morals; we desire it in the family and in society; we may even, while talking about it, profess it for one's self; but in active life it is quite another thing: in a word, we desire humility for all save in ourselves; fresh proof, therefore, that Jesus, who not only proclaimed it, but lived it, was superior to our race, puffed up as it is with pride and vanity. We measure the true greatness of Jesus by his voluntary humility.

The last proof of humility afforded by the life of Jesus, namely, his voluntary death, leads us to the second moral principle which distinguishes his teaching—devotedness. He demands of his disciples that they should forsake all in order to follow him; that they should take up their cross, accept persecutions, and devote themselves, their goods, and their families, to the service of God and of their fellow-creatures. Doubtless this is an admirable principle, and one which all men accept in theory. In practice, however, it is very different. We admire the precept, Serve your brethren; but we practice the proverb, Every one for himself.

What was the conduct of Jesus in this respect? Did he act consistently? We do not now say that he gave his life that our sins might be blotted out, and that he left heaven to come and teach us; no, we might be told that we must first prove that he really did come from heaven. No one, though looking upon Jesus as no more than a superior man, will deny his devotedness. If we may credit M. Renan, Jesus was a transcendent genius, and therefore able to win his way to the highest ranks of society, as so many others have done. On the contrary, he devoted himself entirely to the moral education of the people. In order to accomplish this task he accepted the conflict with the great, whom he unmasked; he incurred their hatred; he voluntarily submitted to the wrongs they did him, to their attacks and their calumnies. When, by a simple recantation, he might have avoided death, he was the first to say, I cannot do it! I am the Son of God. Under the lash and nailed to the cross, he never shrunk from the trial of suffering. It is unnecessary to describe his martyrdom, it is sufficiently well known; but this martyrdom was the most sublime devotedness! Thus, by choosing an obscure life, mostly spent in the streets, while he might have obtained a brilliant career, and have sat in the chair of Moses; by accepting death upon the scaffold when he could have placed himself under the protection of Pilate; by living on alms, teaching the people, exposing himself to scorn, having no prospect of worldly compensation either in the present or in the future, leaving behind him the memory of his name only in the recollections of a few poor men, many of whom probably could scarcely read or write; surely, in the presence of all these facts, it will not be credited that even the most discerning eye has discovered, in such a life, the secret and selfish motive which tarnishes this sublime self-denial!

We now point out two other moral principles, which, though of less frequent application, are yet not the less striking. Jesus, in his sermon on the mount, had taught the forgiveness of injuries; and when Simon Peter asked him, "Lord, how oft shall my brother sin against me, and I forgive him? until seven times?" the reply Jesus gave him was, "I say not unto thee, Until seven times: but, Until seventy times seven." He also said, "Whosoever shall smite thee on thy right cheek, turn to him the other also."

Such is the precept. Did Jesus follow it? Yes; and we venture to add that he went beyond the letter of the precept, and admirably fulfilled it in its spirit. A servant struck him on one cheek: did he turn the other? He did better: without retaliation or complaint, he instructed the man who thus insulted him by calmly answering, "If I have spoken evil, bear witness of the evil: but if well, why smitest thou me?" What dignity and sweetness is here! What a noble lesson! If ever in the course of our life-time we have been, like him, the victims of an undeserved and brutal assault, which flushed our cheeks and clenched our fists in resentment, did it occur to us to say, "If I have spoken evil, bear witness of the evil: but if well, why smitest thou me?" Alas! these are not the words which proceed from our poor humanity under its provocations. In this reply we have the loving spirit, not the dead letter. It is better than forgiveness; it is love, seeking to bring the guilty one to repentance.

On another occasion, Jesus and his Apostles came to a certain village, where they were refused admission by the inhabitants. The Apostles, angry at this insult, asked Jesus to call down fire from heaven upon the guilty place. With his characteristic gentleness the Master replied, "Ye know not what manner of spirit ye are of. For the Son of man is not come to destroy men's lives, but to save them." Here we have the forgiveness of injuries, without pomp or ostentation.

Lastly, Jesus proclaimed a principle which is as universally approved as it is rarely practiced; that, namely, of love for our enemies—"Love your enemies, bless them that curse you, and pray for them which persecute you." The precept is explicit. Did Jesus follow it? We shall judge for ourselves. At Gethsemane he rebukes his disciple who is anxious to avenge him. "Put up again," says he, "thy sword into his place: for all they that take the sword shall perish by the sword." At the gate of Jerusalem, he weeps over the fickle people who would not listen to them: "O Jerusalem, Jerusalem, thou that killest the Prophets, and stonest them which are sent unto thee, how often would I have gathered thy children together, even as a hen gathereth her chickens under her wings, and ye would not!" Though at liberty to defend himself, Jesus remains silent before his enraged foes, Caiaphas, Pilate, and Herod, who seek to entrap him, who insult and strike him. He might have retaliated, and the more so because he was prepared to die. A mere man would have afforded himself the satisfaction of confounding his unjust judges. No, Jesus keeps silence, and this silence reveals as much the calmness of his spirit as the gentleness of his heart.

An arrest, however, is not an execution; mockings do not torture like bearing the cross; this does not *lacerate* like the nails. What will Jesus do when the soldiers, the priests, and the mob unite to abuse him, to laugh him to scorn, to pierce his hands, and to make him drink the cup of bitterness? What will he reply to the taunt of the infatuated crowd, the thieves, and the priests: "If thou be the son of God, come down from the cross. He saved others; himself he cannot save. He trusted in God; let him deliver him now, if he will have him?" Alas! we confess that had we been in his place we should have made a last great effort to come down; and, in our impotence, we should at least have given vent to our fury by throwing back their insults: "Cowards, who mock a condemned man to whose words you but lately listened with admiration! hypocrites, who should at this very hour be purifying yourselves, in the Temple, for the Passover, but who prefer to make yourselves impure by witnessing an execution! worthy sons are ye of your fathers, who in all ages have been executioners and murderers?" Was it thus Jesus spoke to his enemies? No; but addressing God and forgetting himself, he exclaims, "Father, forgive them, for they know not what they do!" To pray for those who tear your flesh, insult your agony, and rail at your devotedness; to excuse them even because of their ignorance—is not this to love your enemies, to bless them that curse you, and to pray for them that persecute you?

Such is the saint whom a critic thinks he honors by transforming into his own image! such is the hero to whom are attributed a "transcendent scorn" and "subtle raillery," and who is styled "a master of irony!" Is it scorn that sparkles in this appeal: "Come unto me, all ye that labor and are heavy laden, and I will give you rest; learn of me, for I am meek and lowly in heart?" Is it derision that we find in these words to the Apostles: "I call you no more servants, but friends: love one another, as I have loved you?" Is there any subtle railing in the prayer: "Our Father who art in heaven, Hallowed be thy name; Thy kingdom come: Thy will be done in earth, as it is in heaven?" Ah, if scorn, mockery, and irony are to be found any where, it is not in the Gospel of Jesus Christ, but in a book which lacks honesty, and dissembles its scorn and its railing under the appearances of respect and admiration; a book whose false praises sweeten the edges of a cup which is full of bitterness and poison.

How deeply we feel that neither our own pen, nor that of any uninspired man, can ever worthily reproduce the character of Jesus Christ. After having so many times vainly attempted it, we despair of success. Have our readers, for instance, ever met with a head of Christ which has satisfied them? We never have. Artists and writers only give us magnified men. Nature furnishes no model which resembles Jesus. The most perfect of these are still essentially men. Alexander, Cesar, Napoleon, all have our passions, though we have not their genius. In Socrates and Plato we discover the germs of our weakness, though they are wiser than we. A St. Paul, an Augustine, and a Pascal, leave us far behind on the road to holiness; yet we recognize them, by means of their defects, as members of our poor human family; and even were we disposed to be too indulgent toward them, their own confessions are there to correct us. Thus, always and every-where, man remains essentially man.

The Evangelists alone have made us conceive an ideal which no man, whether in his life or by his pen, has ever reproduced; and if, as we may well suppose, their picture is as far from the reality, as we are from their copy, what must not the living Christ have been ? *

* It would be interesting to compare the style of the Evangelists with that of M. Renan. In the former we find simplicity and the complete absence of pretense. We have no epithets, no oratorical displays. We forget the writers. It is their hero we have before us, and, what is remarkable, the historian does not eulogize him, but allows us to form our own estimate from the facts themselves. If we except one or two words of St. John's, the four Evangelists have not written a line which reveals any purpose besides that of writing a history. There is no attempt to make the readers proselytes to a cause or a doctrine.

In M. Renan's work all this is reversed. One perceives that the principal thing kept in view is the literary character of the book. The style takes precedence of the facts; elegance is the author's highest ambition. He seems to have imposed upon himself the rule not to write like any other man. All the turns of phrase, all the expressions, aim at the picturesque and the novel. Wit, cleverness, mental reservation, the art of forcing a secret conclusion upon the conclusion which is expressed, and of discrediting the cause which in appearance is defended—such is M. Renan's task. But clever persons sometimes do a work which disappoints them. "The Life of Jesus" has cost its author more moral discredit than all his previous works have obtained for him of literary renown. After eighteen centuries the Gospel is being diffused still; after three months M. Renan's book has materially lost in public opinion. M. Scherer, who on the appearance of the work predicted on its behalf a success so great that it would be felt even by those who never

Jesus resembles no other man; he speaks and acts as none of our kind ever spoke and acted. At first he surprises us, but as we contemplate him, our surprise changes into admiration. The more we examine, the more we discover in his words profound thoughts and lofty sentiments which, till then, had never entered our minds or our hearts. In the midst of his superior world and his superhuman atmosphere, Jesus lives and breathes as in his own element. There he moves freely, he speaks without effort; all is familiar to him—he is at home. Heaven is his country, holiness is his nature, eternity is his life. He does not demonstrate, as we mere men are obliged to do, who have no right to be believed on our simple assertions; he speaks like a God, whose word

heard of it, three months later is obliged to recognize that it has attracted only the curious, and summarizes the well-founded objections made to it thus: 1. M. Renan has judged a moral work in the spirit of a mere artist. 2. He has virtually denied the integrity and the purity of Jesus Christ. 3. He has falsified his character by making of an admirable teacher an unnatural colossus.—*Vide Le Temps, September* 29, 1863.

is law. Nothing embarrasses him ; he speaks of heaven and hell, life and death, the judgment and eternity, as of things he has seen, and which belong to his domain. His constant thought is about the kingdom of God, and he is solely occupied with the will of his Father, and the sanctification of humanity. His feet scarcely touch the earth, his heart is ever in heaven. We feel that he is a stranger to the petty affairs of this world ; even the functions of a secular judge are beneath him ; possibly his hand was never soiled by contact with money. He is simple and humble, but grave. He never utters a jesting word, not even a useless one ; nor does he ever speak in order to display his intellectual superiority. And as a last noteworthy feature, Jesus certainly wept ; but we do not learn that he ever laughed. Yet he never forgot his disciples, nor ever lost sight of the most remote generations of sinners that were to come after him. His thoughts, like his love, embrace the universe. Surely, this is the Son of God !

30

If now we pass from the words to the actions of Jesus, we are filled with the same admiration. It has been asserted that Jesus patronizes the poor and threatens the rich: it would be more truthful to say, that he takes no account of either poverty or riches; gold and stubble are of equal value to him. It is the spiritual condition of those who approach him which claims his attention. What he demands is not lofty thoughts or noble sentiments, but a moral condition which is possible to all. He asks for a heart which, though broken and contrite, yet expects every thing at his hands—healing grace, salvation, and eternal life. When Jesus performs miracles they do not astonish him: he is engaged in his own proper work We may, indeed, reject them without examination; but when we honestly study them, we find it to be quite natural that the Son of God should work such miracles; specially since these miracles have nothing in common with the prodigies of a thaumaturgus, whose aim is to fascinate the eye and to mislead the imagination. The mighty works of Jesus are just what we might expect from a God who created and now sustains us: he gives food, health, life, forgiveness, to all who, in faith, lay their wants before him. Unbeliever, you are surprised, and you do not know what conclusion to draw from these miracles, but you dare not deny them. Be sincere, and confess that there is something in them beyond your apprehension. Believer, you are delighted. These miracles seem to you the natural operations of the Son of God. You learn from them that he gives comfort, healing, and forgiveness. He were not God did he act otherwise. Let but Jesus speak, and your attention is redoubled. His maxims, by penetrating into your spirit, give you light: the more you study them, the more you find them beautiful and brilliant with the light of truth. They are like the starry heavens, which reveal to your earnest gaze new depths, filled with new lights, of which even the most dim are clear. Moreover, that which removes from you the fear of delusion, is the fact that all these marvels have, as their end and aim, not the satisfaction of your curiosity, but the purification of your heart, the raising of your mind, and the kindling of your devotion. Yes; this is the test by which we prove the pure gold of the character of Jesus Christ. It is not possible to contemplate him without moral gain. The glow of life is communicated from him to us: it pervades our being, it blesses and sanctifies us. Jesus is the spiritual Sun that warms and vivifies our souls. No one but a God can make us thus at once better and happier.

We know that all we have said reposes on the authenticity of the Gospels and on the historic fidelity of their narratives. We also know that M. Renan, who admits in general this authenticity and this fidelity, nevertheless contradicts them in their details. We would observe that the authenticity of the Gospels is not at the mercy of any critic, whatever may be his ability. Christianity proves the purity of its root by the excellence of its fruits. If necessary, we might accept the invalidation of the Gospels and of the miracles of Jesus; further still, we might grant that there is no proof of his resurrection, his ascension, and the inspiration of his Apostles: let every thing else be denied, yet we cannot deny what we see to-day. Three hundred millions of men acknowledge Jesus Christ, and the civilization of Christendom exceeds all others both in its extent and its depth. Pure morals; a mild legislation; the raising of woman to her true standard; the freedom of slaves; the relief of the sick, the helpless, and the poor; the brotherhood of nations—these are things before our very eyes, but only to be found in the Christian world. What we ask, therefore, is this: Do all these things exist without cause? Do they date from yesterday? If, in searching for their origin, we must go back to the first century of our era, shall we find them to have been spontaneous growths? Is this transformation without parentage? Did it spring from the previous moral rottenness? Let the divine mission of Jesus Christ, the gift of the Holy Spirit, and the existence of the miracles, be denied; will the void thus made better cxplain the immense results of which we are witnesses than do the evangelical histories? Is Christianity the offspring of a dream? Did it grow in a night? Did humanity wake up one morning and find it already established in the earth? Men are anxious to lessen the causes; but the smaller these are, the more astounding do the results become. By substituting feeble beginnings for great ones we do not destroy the miracle; on the contrary, we make it all the greater. To be rational, then, we must admit a Divine intervention; and this intervention restores to us again the existence of Jesus, his veracity, his miracles, and the whole train of proofs which had been before rejected.

Thus, whatever may be affirmed or denied, actual facts cannot be overturned. The work of Christianity is before us, and the grandeur of its origin is proved both by its nature and its extent. Its sources may be many, but they must be Divine; for man, in his inability to change his own heart, never could have the power to transform the hearts and lives of twenty generations.

It must be understood that we have not pretended, in this short sketch, to trace the entire life of Jesus Christ. To know that life we must read and study the New Testament. Our aim has been to show that the Jesus of the Gospels is not that of M. Renan. His Jesus is a compound of cunning and fanaticism; an imaginary being created for the amusement of novel-readers. The historic Jesus is quite another being; pre-eminently sincere, always calm, profound in his teaching, holy in his conduct, devoted both in life and death, and so much above the greatest men of every age, that we may well believe him when he says, and says again, "I am the Son of God."

THE END.

www.ingramcontent.com/pod-product-compliance
Lightning Source LLC
LaVergne TN
LVHW050520100826
845148LV00002B/400